"Proverbs tells us that whoever walks with the wise becomes wise, and nowhere is that more true than on the amazing journey of being a dad. I'm so thankful for this book full of wise words and thoughts on fatherhood from some wise men (and a wise woman)."

STEVEN CURTIS CHAPMAN
Dad of six; Grammy and Dove Award-winning singer
and songwriter

"This book is wonderfully written, timely, and needed for all men—especially African American men who are daily faced with caring for their fragile families. I highly recommend *The 21-Day Dad's Challenge* and pray the challenges presented will be accepted and put into practice by everyone who reads it."

JOHN PERKINS
Co-founder and chairman of the board, Christian
Community Development Association; president, John
M. Perkins Foundation for Reconciliation and Development

"Would you believe that being a great dad can be fun? You and your child can enjoy growing closer at the ice cream shop, in a church service project, at the pet store, even at the junkyard—and this book shows how. And in only three weeks! The smallest changes can make the biggest difference. Day by day, this book brings you closer to being the dad you really want to be."

GARY SMALLEY
Author, *Change Your Heart, Change Your Life*

"Desiring for decades to parent more effectively, I wish Carey Casey had provided his illuminating book years ago. Fortunately, I can now use its inspiration to become a better father to my adult children and eventually my grandchildren."

BARRY C. BLACK, PH.D.
Chaplain of the United States Senate

THE 21-DAY DAD'S CHALLENGE

THE 21-DAY DAD'S CHALLENGE

THREE WEEKS
TO A
BETTER
RELATIONSHIP
WITH
YOUR KIDS

CAREY CASEY

GENERAL EDITOR

 Tyndale House Publishers, Inc.
Carol Stream, Illinois

Library of Congress Cataloging-in-Publication Data
The 21-day dad's challenge : three weeks to a better relationship with your kids / Carey Casey, general editor.—1st ed.
    p. cm.
"A Focus on the Family book"
Includes bibliographical references.
ISBN 978-1-58997-681-8
1. Fathers—Religious life—Textbooks. 2. Fatherhood—Religious aspects—Christianity—Textbooks. I. Casey, Carey, 1955- II. Title: Twenty-one day dad's challenge. III. Title: Three weeks to a better relationship with your kids.
 BV4529.17.A15 2011
 248.8'421—dc23

                                2011030114

Printed in the United States of America
1 2 3 4 5 6 7 / 16 15 14 13 12 11

CONTENTS

Bonus Challenges

WHAT'S THIS?

Whenever you see a symbol like this in *The 21-Day Dad's Challenge*, it's time to whip out your smartphone if you've got one. Go to your app store and download any free QR code reader and install it. Then scan the code using the camera on your phone. You'll find yourself watching a video with extra encouragement and helpful tips about that day's challenge. Get started by scanning the code on this page for a special introduction to this book.

Note: If you don't have a smartphone, you can view the videos by going to the Web address listed next to each code symbol. For this introduction, that's http://www.21DayDadChallenge.com/Intro.

Dedication

BY CAREY CASEY

This book is dedicated to my friend Peter J. Spokes. He was my partner in leading the National Center for Fathering, and his fingerprints will continue to be very evident in the Center's work. He was a fantastic complement to me, since he had skills in areas where I don't. And although I only knew him for a little more than four years, my respect for him grew just about every day.

That statement held true in the last days of his life, as his body began to shut down after a battle with leukemia and complications of a bone marrow transplant.

He was not perfect by any stretch of the imagination. But I watched him live with a kind of courage that we would all do well to emulate, right up to his last breaths on this earth. His influence on me, and on hundreds if not thousands of others, will not soon be forgotten.

In this brief tribute, I hope you will not only gain an appreciation for who Peter was, but also be challenged and inspired in your own fathering.

First, Peter had *a passionate commitment to help dads*. He served at the National Center for sixteen years, most recently as president and chief operating officer. From the very beginning, this work was a passion and a calling on his life. Why would a Yale graduate with a Stanford MBA and a successful, lucrative career at General Mills leave all that and uproot his wife and six kids to join a small non-profit organization? Because he believed he could help affect the lives of fathers and children. Helping others was a higher priority than serving himself, and it showed in his life every day.

One morning during Peter's final days, I went to see him very early. After we laughed and joked a bit, I told him, "I hate thinking about it, but it seems like you will get your reward before I do."

He just smiled.

I said, "School me up here. From your perspective right now, what do you want to tell me?"

He said, "Carey, if there's anything I would say, it's, 'Finish the work.'"

Dad, even during what had to be the most difficult time of his life, *he had you in mind*. He gave all he could to the cause of inspiring and equipping fathers because he knew this work is strategic in helping children and our society.

Second, Peter had *no regrets*. He was truly a Championship Father. He was a driving force behind much of our work at the Center, and lived out his own personal commitment to his family. He demonstrated for all of us what it means to be a great dad, a father to the fatherless, and a man with a heart for helping other men understand and pursue their role as fathers.

During those last weeks before he died, Peter tried to think of anyone he had offended, anyone from whom he needed to seek forgiveness, or anything important that he had yet to say to someone. He talked to his pastor and continued to meditate and pray about this during those long, lonely hours in the hospital, and *he couldn't think of anyone.* He was one of those rare people who actually kept up with life. He made sure the important things got done.

Judging from everything I saw, Peter invested himself in his family every day. He never let his priorities get off track, so he never had to "make it up" to his wife and children later on. He made sure his family received his best time; he planned ahead and anticipated what his children might need from him, and did his best to meet those needs. He made his kids' academic and spiritual education a high priority, and took an active role in many areas of their lives. He didn't put off difficult talks with a child or avoid addressing family challenges. That kind of faithful, everyday commitment doesn't often make the headlines, but it might be the most courageous thing a father can do.

Even during his last days, through all the pain and difficulties he was experiencing, he was thinking about others and planning ways to help them go on with life. Some people get really mean and selfish when they're sick; often it changes the way they function. But not Peter.

With his family, Peter made sure nothing was left unsaid. He spoke blessings to each of his children and passed on nuggets of wisdom that were important to him. Can you imagine having those conversations with your wife and children? Two of his daughters were not yet married, so he reinforced earlier conversations about what to look for in a husband. He talked to his two unmarried boys about choosing a bride. He gave them all thoughts about how to handle children when they eventually have kids. He talked about working with integrity at their jobs.

And when he did pass away, it was inspiring to see how his family members were there for each other. They responded as positively as you could ever expect. I believe it's largely due to the fact that Peter had spent years laying a foundation of love, respect, and integrity. He'd helped family members form strong communication habits, so they were much more able to handle his illness and his passing.

I still hurt for Peter and his family. I wanted them all to be able to share many more years together. I wanted him to help all his kids get married, see his grandbabies come into the world, the whole nine yards. I know that what he's doing now is much better than even those things, but I wish he could have done them.

His family tree didn't have a long history of faith. But Peter made a courageous choice to trust God and go deep with Him. I know his faith carried him through his most difficult moments. He said his greatest joy was knowing that all six of his children—and two more by marriage—loved the Lord Jesus Christ. There's really nothing more important for a father than that.

I appreciate you reading about my friend, whom I still miss just about every day. But I also hope you'll take something from this dedication that you can use. Since funerals and memorials are for the benefit of the living, it's appropriate to ask, "What about you, dad?"

Are you pursuing Championship Fathering—loving, coaching, and modeling for your children, encouraging other children, and enlisting other dads to get involved? Are you investing yourself in causes greater than yourself? Or are you making the mistake of thinking you'll make priority changes next week or next year?

Like Peter, let's make sure that every day we leave nothing unsaid or undone with our wife and children.

ACKNOWLEDGMENTS

Looking at the list of people who contributed chapters to this book, I am humbled and inspired. It's an impressive group. But even more than that, it's a sign that more and more people are joining the Championship Fathering movement to inspire and equip dads. So I thank all those whose names are listed in the Table of Contents, who are helping to give voice and bring momentum to the movement.

Thankfully, the movement is bigger than just this book. We definitely need more voices than mine, and there are many others I should mention. Those include:

- Jim Daly and our friends at Focus on the Family, especially Larry Weeden and John Duckworth, who truly made this book happen; and Tyndale House Publishers for their long and supportive relationship with the National Center for Fathering.

- Others who are part of the national fatherhood movement, including our partners and friends at the National Fatherhood Leaders Group; the White House Office of Faith-Based and Neighborhood Partnerships; the National Association of Basketball Coaches; Sherwood Pictures and others involved in the movie *Courageous*; and a growing list of professional athletes and coaches who are helping to promote responsible fatherhood.

- Our dedicated staff and board at the National Center for Fathering and our WATCH D.O.G.S. team, many of whom were instrumental in this book project, and all of whom are great encouragements to me. For projects like this one,

I want to mention Brock Griffin, who helps to capture my thoughts and turn them into useful pieces for dads.

- My family members, without whom my own fathering journey would have very little meaning. My bride, Melanie, supports me in so many ways—especially through her prayers—so I can continue doing what I do. Thanks also to my children: Christie Hammond, Patrice Perkins, Marcellus Casey, Chance Casey, and their spouses and children. I am also grateful for our family heritage—our parents, the Caseys and the Littles.

There are others I would like to mention, but I can't—because there isn't space here or I simply don't know their names. They are everyday dads who are being faithful in their commitments to their families. They are fathers, grandfathers, and father figures who volunteer at their children's schools as WatchDOGS. They are women who support and forgive their husbands and other men in their journeys to be good dads. They are men and women who volunteer to help us carry out our work with fathers at our events or in our offices.

These are also part of the movement, and I am once again humbled and grateful. They are taking action and trying to make a difference, and that's what our society and our world truly needs.

CAREY CASEY

Introduction

BY CAREY CASEY

Snap on your chin strap, dad. You're about to be hit with some powerful insights that will inspire and equip you to be the father your children need.

I hope you'll get used to the idea that a better father is on the other side of reading this book. Whether your fathering needs minor adjustments or a radical overhaul, start preparing for it now. Allow God to work in your life through His Word and the experiences that have helped to shape me and the other authors of this book. Soak in the fatherly wisdom and take full advantage of the challenges and the action planning exercises included in each chapter.

I'm humbled and grateful to be part of the writing team with these other men (and a woman). These are people I greatly respect and admire. There's even one chapter by a young man who saw the best and the worst moments of my own fathering—my son Marcellus. You probably can imagine the fear and trepidation I felt as I read his chapter. But he did a fantastic job, along with the others who are part of this project.

I'm confident that you—and your children, and *their* children—

will receive benefits and blessings because you picked up this book. Your involved fathering will make a lasting difference.

Allow me to share a larger perspective for you to keep in mind before you start filling your brain with these twenty-one great ideas.

I always say that the things that will change our society don't cost a lot of money or require new ideas from the sharpest minds. Mostly, effectiveness in life is about being faithful with the basics—following through on the bedrock values and priorities that are truly meaningful.

It's the same with your family. According to our research, you can have a great impact on your children through simple acts of loving, coaching, and modeling—the three fundamentals of Championship Fathering. I know being a dad is a challenge, but it isn't rocket science. A simple approach will help you do your best.

When I see or hear about a dad doing simple but outstanding things—like helping his child with music lessons—I'm inspired. When I see a father and child playing a board game together, I think it's incredible! I'm moved when I drive on the freeway and see a father talking with his daughter, both of them smiling and laughing in the lane next to me.

It's the simple things that matter: reading Bible stories, going fishing, watching a movie and eating popcorn together, talking about the day, having a water fight, building something together, helping with homework, telling jokes, watching the sun go down. The possibilities are limited only by a child's imagination and a dad's willingness to go with the flow.

My bride, Melanie, and I have four children. Our three oldest—two daughters and a son—are married and raising amazing grandchildren. My youngest son, Chance, is a teenager. Being in my fifties, it isn't easy, let me tell you! But I'm convinced that one of the reasons God gave us Chance at our age is to remind me of the simple things. I try to join him outside and play, just like any other dad. We read a chapter of Proverbs every morning; we fix breakfast together. Although I played football, Chance enjoys tennis, so I often practice with him. Some days I sit outside in the grass with him, just doing whatever he wants at the time. More than anything, I'm trying to be there on a daily basis. It's all everyday, simple stuff.

I believe one of the reasons God gives us children—at any age— is to help us learn to appreciate the value of the small, uncomplicated things of life. From an eternal perspective, what could we possibly do that's better than hanging out in the backyard with a son or daughter, going on a family picnic or bike ride, helping a child look at leaves under a microscope, or lying on the grass at night and looking up at the stars?

Over time, making those simple investments in your children will have the biggest effect. I don't mean to imply that "simple" is synonymous with "easy." Fathering does require some sacrifice. You will be asked to give up or delay some things that you enjoy, and that's never a breeze. In truth, though, "sacrifice" probably isn't the best word for this, because you and other dedicated fathers will probably view this as a wise trade because that's where your priorities are. What you're asked to give up isn't nearly as important as your critical role in your children's lives. Making those eternal investments is what you're all about; the benefits far outweigh the costs.

I know one dad who made a commitment to get up at 5 A.M. every day so he could practice basketball with his son. He wanted to help his son chase a dream, and that was the time when it worked for both of them. That son eventually earned a college scholarship to play basketball.

Another dad, one of our master trainers at the National Center, took up fencing because it was an area of interest for his son and there was no local program for young boys. This father joined the adults' fencing club and then helped his son learn the sport. Through the years they continued to practice together and began traveling to competitions. More than ten years later, they coach each other—talking strategy, offering encouragement, pointing out ways they can improve, and celebrating victories. They've traveled to major fencing events in the U.S. and abroad, and both have earned great accolades.

Neither of those dads came up with revolutionary parenting approaches; they just made commitments that asked them to stretch and adjust, and did so willingly. Today they aren't looking back and thinking about what they gave up for their kids; they're happy for the memories they made. They overcame obstacles and found ways to invest in their children's lives. Their actions were simple and heroic.

I'm convinced that if we make that kind of commitment to do the simple things as fathers, we can transform our families for the better. Collectively we truly can have an impact on a culture where, according to statistics, more and more kids are at risk—and the future for children looks ominous.

I pray that these twenty-one tips will be useful in shaping your fathering habits, even if only ten or twelve really resonate with you or fit where you are as a dad. Make the most of the great ideas and inspiration you find here. But keep in mind that your simple, everyday commitment is likely to have the greatest influence on your fathering.

You don't have to fix everything or have all the answers. Your children need you to *just be Dad*.

As much as anything else, they need to know you're committed to them—and that no matter how challenging fatherhood may be, nothing can change that.

The Fun of Fatherhood

BY CAREY CASEY

My son Chance is now a teenager, which brings its own set of joys and challenges. A lot of things are changing—for him *and* for me. Some days we get along great, but of course we have our share of tension and disagreements. Some days he's a knucklehead, and I know I am too at times. So I need to be *balanced* as I relate to him.

On one side is the fun. To help maintain a strong relationship, I've started a regular routine on school days. He goes out in front of our house to wait for the bus; I grab a cup of coffee and join him for a few minutes while he's waiting. He's a captive audience then, and it's a great opportunity to check in, ask him a few questions, and just be together.

Oh, yeah, I should probably mention . . . I do all this while *still wearing my bathrobe.*

So, as the minutes pass, he'll get this look on his face and just stare at me.

"What's wrong, Son?" I'll ask.

He'll say, "I'm waiting for you to go back in the house."

He never enjoys my mischievous smile at this point. "Dad," he'll say, "don't stand out here! The bus is coming around the corner in a few seconds."

It's probably Chance's biggest fear right now that I—his out-of-touch father—would embarrass him more than I already have. If I ever stayed outside in my bathrobe when the bus pulled up—or maybe went to the curb and waved to all his classmates—his life would be over right then and there. So I always manage to be back in the house before the bus gets close.

But, don't you know, I like to have some fun with it. On my way back in the house, I'll flirt with that front door a little bit. "Hmm. You think they could see me if I stood *here*? How about *here*?"

He'll say, "Dad, *don't*!" But he knows I'm just having fun. And I know he'll find other ways to get back at me.

Isn't it part of a father's job to embarrass his kids? Did your father do that? Since we're going to be uncool for a few years in our kids' eyes, we may as well have a little fun with it, right? It's okay to pick them up from school in the oldest car we have, blasting classic rock or R&B out the windows, or start the wave at the next sports event. Maybe we could even wear our favorite Hawaiian shorts around their friends, or pull out the baby album when they bring a date home for dinner.

I do believe we need to have a lot of fun with our kids, and humor will actually help them develop higher creative and coping skills. There's even room for some good-natured teasing, as long as we're sensitive to the possibility of going too far and becoming mean-spirited.

That's the other side—the humility we need to show our kids. Not long ago, I was joking around with Chance and I did go too far. I said something in fun that I later realized had cut deeper. So I went back to him and said, "Son, Daddy has to ask for your forgiveness.

The words I said to you this morning and how I said them were not right, and I'm sorry. I have to be more discerning and more sensitive to what you're going through."

As we relate to our children and coach them to be responsible, God-fearing adults, there's a lot of room for humor, energy, and fun. Those activities bring more interest and excitement to life, and they provide great bonding opportunities. But we must balance this with self-control and humility. Balanced fathering should be our goal.

I believe that kind of balance is part of what Paul had in mind when he wrote in Ephesians 6:4, "Fathers, do not exasperate your children; instead, bring them up in the training and instruction of the Lord."

Dads who don't have fun with their kids will exasperate them. If my fathering is always about making sure my son behaves or performs to a certain standard, he'll be frustrated and want to give up. More than once there's been no patience or kindness in my voice when I've said to him, "Chance, why isn't your room clean?" Or, "Son, why do you continue to do that when I told you it needs to be done *this* way?"

I often stand in front of dads' groups and say things like, "Don't sweat the small stuff. There are more important things than a clean room." Then I'll forget my own advice when I get home. Sure, Chance has to get better at some things—but I should know better, too.

I guess it shows I'm doing okay when I tuck him into bed at night and he reaches out his arms and says, "Dad, I need a hug." There's nothing quite like it.

But then, don't you know, the next morning we'll be in front of our house, me in my bathrobe and Chance giving me that anxious look—with a hint of a smile behind it.

It's good to be a dad.

YOUR CHALLENGE

Are you willing to try something new as you seek to have fun with your kids? Use your imagination! Being able to laugh with them—and at yourself—could open up new lines of communication and make you more approachable when serious matters arise.

A good place to start is to hang out in their world, figuring out what tickles their funny bone. During the next 24 hours, notice the kinds of things they and their friends are laughing at. As long as it's clean, join in. Read something humorous that your child likes to read, watch a video he thinks is funny, or check out a Web site she finds amusing.

YOUR PLAN

Use the following space to list three things you can look at, listen to, and laugh about with your child during the next day or so. Then write down some thoughts about these questions:

Would your kids say that you're a "fun" dad? Why or why not?

What routines or activities might be likely to bring out the joking or playful side of your personality more often?

What areas of your child's life are off limits when it comes to making jokes? If you're not sure, talk with your child's mom or someone else who knows him or her well. If you and your child have a history of "misunderstood" teasing or unappreciated pranks, chances are good that you both need to make some changes. How can you do your part?

_____

_____

_____

_____

_____

_____

_____

■ ■ ■

CAREY CASEY is CEO of the National Center for Fathering, head-quartered in Kansas City, and the author (with Neil Wilson) of *Championship Fathering: How to Win at Being a Dad.* Speaking across the U.S. and around the world, Carey encourages and equips men to be the fathers their children need. He has served as a chaplain for NFL football teams and the U.S. Olympic team, and as an inner-city pastor in Chicago. For eighteen years Carey was on staff with the Fellowship of Christian Athletes, serving as national urban director and president of the FCA Foundation. Carey and his wife, Melanie, have four children and five grandchildren.

For more help in taking today's challenge, scan the symbol with your smartphone. See instructions on page xi in the front of this book. Or visit http://www.21DayDadChallenge.com/Day1.

DAY 2

Where Closeness Comes From

BY JOSH D. MCDOWELL

There are no guarantees. None! You can be the greatest father in the world and do everything right, but there's absolutely no guarantee that your child won't grow up and walk away from you or walk away from his or her faith.

If you build a *relationship* with that child, though, the chance of that ultimate rebellion happening is very small. What usually brings a child back is not all the truth you've taught but what kind of relationship you've built.

You may be experiencing a rocky relationship with your child right now, but it's never too late to start where you are. We must connect with our kids *relationally* to overcome their resistance to our guidance and instruction.

We can apply biblical principles that provide relational connecting points to meet real needs in our kids' lives. These seven points help ready our young people mentally, emotionally, and spiritually to receive our advice about right thinking and behavior—thus avoiding the traps of the culture around them.

1. *Affirmation.* One of the most effective ways of identifying with your children, even when you don't fully understand them, is

to affirm their feelings. To affirm means to "validate or confirm." *When we affirm the feelings of our young people, we give them a sense of authenticity.*

"Rejoice with those who rejoice; mourn with those who mourn" (Romans 12:15). Affirming their feelings tells them they're real individuals with valid feelings. When we identify with their excitement or disappointment, we let them know that we care and that they're understood for who they really are—authentic human beings.

2. *Acceptance.* Your acceptance helps your kids believe that you will still love them no matter what happens. Acceptance is embracing people for who they are rather than for what they do. *When we accept young people for who they are, we give them a sense of security.*

"Accept one another, then, just as Christ accepted you, in order to bring praise to God" (Romans 15:7). When your young people feel accepted by you, they're more likely to be vulnerable and transparent, opening up greater trust between you and your child.

3. *Appreciation.* While acceptance is the foundation for a secure relationship, appreciation can be considered a cornerstone. Appreciation shows young people they're valued and that their accomplishments make a difference. *When we express appreciation to our kids, we give them a sense of significance—the feeling or thought that they've done or said something worthwhile.*

"And a voice from heaven said, 'This is my Son, whom I love; with him I am well pleased'" (Matthew 3:17). Accepting young people tells them that their *being* matters; expressing appreciation to them says that their *doing* matters, too. Catch your children doing something right and show appreciation. I'm convinced that the more I caught my three daughters and son doing things right and expressed appreciation, the less there was to catch them doing wrong.

4. *Affection.* Expressing affection to our kids through loving words and appropriate touch communicates that they're worth loving. *When we show affection to young people, we give them a sense of lovability.*

"Dear friends, let us love one another, for love comes from God. Everyone who loves has been born of God and knows God" (1 John 4:7). Every expression of care and closeness provides emotional reinforcement, helping kids realize that they're loved.

Affection can be expressed through words and appropriate physical contact. We can say "I love you" to our children in a variety of verbal ways—which I made my goal to do with each of my children, either in person or over the phone, ten times a day. Appropriate physical expression is conveyed through a hug, kiss, peck on the cheek, arm around the shoulder, embrace, or holding your child's hand.

5. *Availability.* Expressing affirmation, acceptance, appreciation, and affection to our kids is critical, but we can do that only if we make ourselves available to them. *When we make ourselves available to our children, we give them a sense of importance in our lives.*

"The LORD is near to all who call on him, yes, to all who call on him in truth" (Psalm 145:18). When we're not available, we're saying in essence, "Yes, I love you, but other things still come ahead of you." You see, kids spell love *T-I-M-E.*

My wife, Dottie, is the wisest woman I know. Once when my children were young, she lovingly confronted me and said, "Honey, you're not available to our children. You don't spend time with them, and you will deeply regret it later in life."

She went on to offer what I think is some of the greatest wisdom a person has ever shared with me. She said, "If you spend time with your children now, they'll spend time with you later. If you love them now, they'll love you later. If you talk to them now, they'll listen to you later. If you listen to your children now, they will talk to you later. If you hug them now, they will hug you later."

Being there when your kids need you not only tells them they're important to you; it keeps you relationally connected to them.

6. *Approach.* We need to find out what is significant to our kids, no matter how old they are (it changes with age, of course). Then we need to step into—approach—that world. God, through Jesus, approached our world; we need to apply that same principle with our young people. *When we approach our children's world, we say to them, "I care about you and what interests you."*

"Love is patient, love is kind. . . . It is not self-seeking" (1 Corinthians 13:4-5). When we step into our kids' world, it shows them we care about what they care about. That's the beginning of family and relationships.

7. *Accountability.* To connect relationally with our children, we need to show them affirmation, acceptance, appreciation, affection, availability, and a sincere enthusiasm to approach their world. Still, if we don't balance these relational connecting points with loving limits and boundaries, young people won't learn responsibility. *When we provide loving accountability to our young people, we give them a sense of responsibility.*

"So then, each of us will give an account of himself to God" (Romans 14:12). Accountability provides the parameters within which a young person can operate safely and securely. Young people need the loving authority of parents and other caring adults so they can learn to make responsible, right choices. Sadly, without parameters, there is only confusion and chaos.[1]

YOUR CHALLENGE

How's your relationship with your child? Which of the seven connecting points in this chapter seems most likely to help?

Choose *one* of the points—affirmation, acceptance, appreciation, affection, availability, approach, or accountability. Decide how you'll spend *half an hour out of the next 24* working on that aspect of your relationship.

Here are some ideas to get you started:

1. Affirm your child by asking what was the hardest thing he or she had to do last week—and listening carefully to the answer, recognizing and validating the feelings he or she expresses.

2. Accept your child by *not* mentioning something that usually prods you to complain about him or her—a hairstyle, a tone of voice, a messy room, or an annoying habit.

3. Appreciate your child by noticing something he or she has done right in the last week—and by recognizing that achievement with a homemade certificate or plastic trophy purchased at a party store.

4. Show affection to your child by expressing it verbally a dozen times in the space of thirty minutes.

5. Be available to your child by canceling something you enjoy regularly yourself (watching a newscast, working out, drinking coffee) and replacing it with a father-child activity your son or daughter likes (watching a cartoon, shooting hoops, having a tea party with stuffed animals).

6. Approach your child's world by listening to some of his or her favorite music together.

7. Hold your child accountable by setting a deadline for a chore—and then helping him or her meet it.

YOUR PLAN

In the space below, describe what you'll do and when you'll do it. Do you need to prepare? For instance, if you're going to say something affectionate a dozen times in thirty minutes, you might want to list some ideas.

Consider coming up with a long-range plan, too. If you'll be moving on to a different challenge tomorrow, you may want to practice the other six principles in this chapter when the 21-Day Challenge is over.

_____

_____

_____

_____

_____

_____

_____

_____

_____

_____

_____

_____

■ ■ ■

JOSH MCDOWELL is a popular author and speaker who has addressed more than ten million young people, giving more than 24,000 talks in 118 countries. Since 1961, he has written or co-authored more than 120 books including *The Unshakable Truth: How You Can Experience the 12 Essentials of a Relevant Faith* (with son Sean) and the bestselling *More Than a Carpenter* and *New Evidence that Demands a Verdict.* He and his wife, Dottie, have four children and five grandchildren.

DAY 3

Do the Things Your Kids Want to Do

BY TONY DUNGY

*"Finish your outdoor work and get your
fields ready; after that, build your house."*
PROVERBS 24:27

As a football coach and now a TV commentator, I work long hours and travel a lot. Doing my job and providing for my family often limits the time I'm able to spend with my wife and children.

I've found, though, that the key to getting the most out of our time when we *are* together is my willingness to do what my kids want to do—even when they're not necessarily the things I'd prefer to do.

I'm not talking about big, expensive productions like trips to Disney World or vacations in Hawaii. I'm talking about normal, everyday activities like walks in the park, playing on a swing set, or throwing a football around in the backyard.

Speaking of football . . . as you can imagine, after a very long and exhausting day of coaching, tossing the pigskin around with my boys for another hour after work wasn't usually my idea of fun. (It's like being an insurance adjuster and finding that your child wants you to work on actuarial tables with him at night.) But it was often what they wanted to do, and my willingness to do it let them know they were important to me; if I could do that at work, I should certainly be able to do it for them!

I saw the truth of this with one of my daughters, too, when I heard a friend of hers ask about me. My child didn't say anything about my job or going to NFL games or getting to meet famous athletes that I work with. Instead she said, "He plays Marco Polo in the pool with me." (We live in Florida.) That told me I was doing something right.

Many times when I was coaching, I'd take the boys to the office with me on a Saturday morning. They might play on the practice fields or use my office equipment to play their video games. I knew they liked being with me—but they also liked stopping for donuts on the way home. To tell the truth, I think sometimes they saw the trip to the office as just part of the process of getting to the donut shop! But we have lots of great memories of time spent together in both places.

My wife, Lauren, has been a great help in this area. I recall her saying many times when I returned from a long road trip and she was hungry for time with me herself, "Let's do something the kids will enjoy." So instead of the two of us going to a quiet restaurant, we would head to the park or on a family bike ride—or maybe just to our backyard pool for another game of Marco Polo.

In the evenings during the school year, time is at a premium. There are so many things that have to get done, like homework and chores and bedtime preparations. In the little "together time" we have, I've learned to emphasize the kids' interests. So with one or more children, I may find myself playing a computer game, watching "VeggieTales," or listening to one of their favorite CDs.

I mentioned earlier that I don't always *feel* like doing what my kids want to do. I may be tired, uninspired, and just want a little "down time" for myself. But it may encourage you to know that when I'm feeling that way, and I go ahead and push myself to do the thing they're eager to do, those often become some of our *best* times together. Once I get going on that bike ride or game of catch or computer contest, it's as if I catch a second wind and start to feel rejuvenated. I don't know how psychologists would describe this phenomenon, but I've seen it happen time after time. I take it as God's affirmation that I'm doing a good thing.

I'm busy, and I have a job that requires a lot. But what dad doesn't, especially these days when employees are being asked by their companies to be more productive than ever? That's what I see in Proverbs 24:27, where it tells us to "finish your outdoor work and get your fields ready." Our work is important, and we have an obligation to our employers.

The rest of that verse goes on to say, however, "after that, build your house." To me that's a reminder not to neglect the rest of my calling as a man. We build our houses by taking care of the needs of those within—our wives and children. A big part of that is doing the things *they* want to do in the time we have together day by day.

So here's my suggestion to you: Even though you don't have as much time with your children as you spend on the job, work as hard at your parenting as you do in the office or factory. Give your kids as much effort as you give your employer.

And realize that some days—maybe a lot of days—just as you need to work through some tough challenges on the job, you may need to do some things with your kids in the evening that wouldn't be your first choice. But they're the things your children want to do with you, and going along with their plans is the best way you can say, "I love you, and you're so very important to me."

That's our job as dads, and it's also our privilege.

 YOUR CHALLENGE

Within the next 24 hours, enjoy one of your child's favorite activities with him or her. If you don't know what those activities might be, ask your child! Here are some ideas to get you started:

- Bake something together—perhaps using a recipe your child came up with—and share it with the rest of the family.
- Go to the library and check out a book of science experiments or magic tricks and follow the instructions for the one that interests your child the most.
- Play a basketball-shooting game of "HORSE," but spell your child's full name instead.
- Build a replica of your home (or your child's dream house) out of blocks, LEGOs, toothpicks, or graham crackers and cake icing.
- Rent a DVD of a TV series your child likes and let him or her pick a favorite episode to watch together. (There are plenty of great Christian videos to choose from.)
- If you have a teen who's learning to drive, let him or her chauffer you to a restaurant for pizza; he or she gets to pick the toppings and the radio station you play in the car.

- Act out a Bible story for the rest of the family, but change the setting (and costumes and makeup) to outer space.
- Go to a pet store and let your child come up with names for a dozen of the animals based on their personalities.

YOUR PLAN

In the following space, name three things your child likes to do with you. Try to think of at least one that's not *your* personal favorite.

_____

_____

_____

_____

Which of these three things will you do with your child tonight?

_____

_____

_____

_____

If you need to make any special preparations (make a reservation, find a bicycle pump, withdraw money from your bank account), list them here.

_____

_____

_____

_____

■ ■ ■

Tony Dungy is the *New York Times* bestselling author of *Quiet Strength*, *Uncommon*, and *The Mentor Leader*. As head coach of the Indianapolis Colts, he led his team to victory in the 2007 Super Bowl. He has held coaching positions with the Tampa Bay Buccaneers, Pittsburgh Steelers, Kansas City Chiefs, Minnesota Vikings, and University of Minnesota—and played three seasons in the NFL. Since retiring from coaching in 2009, he has served as a studio analyst for NBC's *Football Night in America*. He and his wife, Lauren, are the parents of seven children.

For more help in taking today's challenge, scan the symbol with your smartphone. See instructions on page xi in the front of this book. Or visit http://www.21DayDadChallenge.com/Day3.

Where's Daddy?

BY DR. GARY ROSBERG

I was sitting in my favorite chair, studying for the final stages of my doctoral degree, when Sarah announced herself in my presence with a question: "Daddy, do you want to see my family picture?"

"Sarah, Daddy's busy. Come back in a little while, Honey."

Good move, right? I was busy. A week's worth of work to squeeze into a weekend. You've been there.

Ten minutes later she swept back into the living room. "Daddy, let me show you my picture."

The heat went up around my collar. "Sarah," I said, "come back later. This is important."

Three minutes later she stormed into the living room, got three inches from my nose, and barked with all the power a five-year-old can muster: "Do you want to see it or don't you?" This was the assertive woman in training.

"No," I told her, "I don't."

With that, she zoomed out of the room and left me alone. And somehow, being alone at that moment wasn't as satisfying as I thought it would be. I felt like a jerk. (Don't agree so loudly.)

I went to the front door. "Sarah," I called, "could you come back inside a minute, please? Daddy would like to see your picture."

She obliged with no recriminations and popped up on my lap.

It was a great picture. She'd even given it a title. Across the top, in her best printing, she had inscribed: OUR FAMILY BEST.

"Tell me about it," I said.

"Here is Mommy [a stick figure with long, yellow, curly hair], here is me standing by Mommy [with a smiley face], here is our dog Katie, and here is Missy [her little sister was a stick figure lying in the street in front of the house, about three times bigger than anyone else]." It was a pretty good insight into how she saw our family.

"I love your picture, Honey," I told her. "I'll hang it on the dining room wall, and each night when I come home from work and from class [which was usually around 10 P.M.], I'm going to look at it."

She took me at my word, beamed ear to ear, and went outside to play. I went back to my books. But for some reason I kept reading the same paragraph over and over.

Something was making me uneasy.

Something about Sarah's picture.

Something was missing.

I went to the front door. "Sarah," I called, "could you come back inside a minute, please? I want to look at your picture again, Honey."

Sarah crawled back into my lap. I can close my eyes right now and see the way she looked. Cheeks rosy from playing outside. Pigtails, Strawberry Shortcake tennis shoes. A Cabbage Patch doll named Nellie tucked limply under her arm.

I asked my little girl a question, but I wasn't sure I wanted to hear the answer.

"Honey . . . there's Mommy, and Sarah, and Missy. Katie the dog is in the picture, and the sun, and the house, and squirrels and birdies. But, Sarah . . . where is your daddy?"

"You're at the library," she said.

With that simple statement, my little princess stopped time for me. Lifting her gently off my lap, I sent her back to play in the spring sunshine. I slumped back in my chair with a swirling head and blood pumping furiously through my heart. Even as I type these words into the computer, I can feel those sensations all over again. It was a frightening moment.

Sarah's simple pronouncement—"You're at the library"—got my attention big-time.

I hung the drawing on the dining room wall, just as I'd promised my girl. And through those long, intense weeks preceding the oral defense of my dissertation, I stared at that revealing portrait. It happened every night in the silence of my home as the rest of the family slept, as I consumed my late-night, warmed-over dinners. I didn't have the guts to bring the issue up to my wife, Barb. And she had the incredible insight to let it rest until I had the courage to deal with it.

Finally I finished my degree program. I was "Dr. Rosberg" now, and I guess it should have been a big deal for me. But frankly, there wasn't much joy in my life.

One night after graduation, Barb and I were lying in bed together. I found myself working up the nerve to ask her a few questions. It was late, it was dark, and as I murmured my first question, I was praying Barb had already fallen asleep.

"Barb, are you sleeping?" I asked.

"No," she said.

Rats! I thought. *Now I'm committed.*

"Barb, you've obviously seen Sarah's picture taped on the dining room wall. Why haven't you said anything?"

"Because I know how much it wounded you, Gary." Words from a woman wise beyond her twenty-something years.

At that point, I asked the toughest question I've ever asked anyone in my life. "Barb . . . I want to come home. Can I do it?"

Twenty seconds of silence followed. It seemed like I held my breath for an hour.

At last Barb spoke. "Gary," she said carefully, "the girls and I love you very much. We want you home. But you haven't been here. I've felt like a single parent for years."

The words look cold in print, but she said them with restraint and tenderness. It was just plain, unvarnished truth. My little girl had drawn the picture, and now her mom was speaking the words. My life had been out of control, my family was on automatic pilot, and I had a long road ahead of me if I wanted to win them back.

But I had to win them back. It suddenly became the most important thing in my life.

For the next two years I served my way home. Games of Candy Land with Missy. Vegetable sandwiches with Sarah. Date nights with Barb.

Two years later, I received the greatest gift a dad could ever experience: another family portrait. I was in the middle of this new picture, which now hangs in my office. It's the story of a family's redemption through the broken heart of a dad and the gracious hearts of the three most important women in my life.

You've probably heard the story of the prodigal son. When he came to his senses, he said, "How many of my father's hired men have food to spare, and here I am starving to death! I will set out and go back to my father and say to him: Father, I have sinned against heaven and against you. I am no longer worthy to be called your son; make me like one of your hired men" (Luke 15:17-19). Well, in my story, I was the prodigal and my family represented the forgiving father.

Come home, dad.

Life is short!

YOUR CHALLENGE

Can you choose to put your family ahead of anything else going on in your life? Can you decide you'll be home instead of spending extra time at the office, on the golf course, or at the library?

Decide that when you have to be away from family members, you'll make sure they understand they're the most important people in your life—and that you're making every effort to be home. Then do whatever you can to get there.

Start by planning a family date—not just with your wife if you're married, but for the kids, too. If you can't schedule it during the next 24 hours, make it as soon as possible. Choose an activity that your kids will love, and that will let you make some fun, new memories together.

YOUR PLAN

In the following space, write down a few available days for your family date. Where would you like to go? What would you like to do? More importantly, what would the rest of the family like?

List several ideas for your family date. Then, if you're married, let your wife make the final choice. If you're not, let the kids decide![2]

_____

_____

_____

_____

_____

_____

_____

_____

■ ■ ■

DR. GARY and BARB ROSBERG are award-winning authors, popular radio hosts, and beloved marriage conference speakers. Together, they are co-founders of the international ministry America's Family Coaches. Through a unique program called The Great Marriage Experience, the Rosbergs equip couples, churches, and military marriages with the resources, events, and tools they need to keep their marriages growing stronger for a lifetime. The Rosbergs live outside Des Moines, Iowa. Married since 1975, they have two married daughters and seven grandchildren.

DAY 5

There's No Place Like Home

BY JOE WHITE

You would have thought the Wizard of Oz tornado had returned to Kansas when a recent Wichita newspaper hit the streets. The business community buzzed like a beehive with questions and speculations about the following headline:

BALDWIN TRADES PRESIDENCY FOR POPS

The most powerful banking chain in Kansas had lost its brilliant, entrepreneurial president overnight. Like Dorothy and Toto, the Scarecrow, the Lion, and the Tin Man, Ron Baldwin had found a new yellow brick road to follow.

Dorothy's road led to Oz and the wizard's rewards for her three newfound friends. Ron's road led to his family and the rewards of spending time with his new grandson and helping his children with their clothing business.

On this one thing Ron and Dorothy agree: "There's no place like home!"

Throughout our culture men are reevaluating priorities, schedules, core values, and company standards. While few of us have the freedom to resign and "run to Oz," countless dads—from CEOs to hourly temps, white collar to blue collar, high-profile leaders to behind-the-scenes support staff—are asking difficult questions. How should they invest their most precious asset of personal time, and their most valuable resource of personal energy?

My work as a sports camp director and motivational speaker brings me alongside thousands of men each year. Whether it's "one on ten thousand" for thirty-five minutes in a Men at the Cross venue, "one on thirty" for twenty minutes in an NFL pre-game locker room, or "one on one" for four hours in a golf cart, what I hear never changes. Good dads care more for their God and their families than for any other aspect of their lives. Most of us, like Ron, are looking for ways to enrich our days by adding more time with those we love the most.

One of my favorite pre-game "spiritual pep talk" stops along the speaking trail is the Oklahoma Sooners football team. That's where head coach Bob Stoops finds himself in the National Championship more times than not. Bob's M.O. for his coaching staff may surprise you. Dorothy and Toto would be pleased, though.

No coach who's a dad is welcome in Bob's office until 9 A.M. To Bob, a coach/dad's favorite offensive formation is made up of wife and kids; his first line of defense is a solid, steady home. Work comes after the kids have been fed breakfast and personally ushered off to school.

This philosophy has helped win diamond-studded National Championship rings for Stoops and his staff. It also secures their humble gold wedding bands, whose value far exceeds the booty from the Orange Bowl and the fickle New Year's Day crowds who attend the games.

Unlike Bob, some of us are slower learners. Yesterday I had a call from a desperate dad whose high profile in his profession has taken him away from home for one too many days. Months and months of travel have cost him his marriage. Now his son, who has begged for attention for fifteen years, is getting it—by teaming up with the wrong friends and forming patterns of dangerous behavior. Today that dad is rearranging his priorities.

That father soon will learn what I learned the hard way twenty-five years ago, when my four kids cried out for my spiritual leadership in our home. I was way too busy and far too preoccupied when I came home at night.

But I did learn. I found out that, as the saying goes, "It's never too late to start. It's always too early to quit."

Scripture is crystal clear on this subject. God's principles for success and fulfillment are unwavering. As sure as He knows every breath we take and sees every hair that falls from our ever-depleting scalps, He calls us to spiritually lead our homes as the carpenter from Nazareth would—by washing feet, carrying a rugged cross, modeling impeccable integrity, and giving our lives for those who follow us.

The crucifixion was no easy way to die. Being spiritual leaders in our homes is no easy way to live.

But is it worth it? I saw the answer to that yesterday, as I returned home from the doctor's office. I'd just had a biopsy that would reveal whether I had prostate cancer. My grown kids called or came by our house to offer their prayers and their love. That made every second of my redirected life worth it—every painful effort to set new priorities and act on them.

When it comes time to leave this earth, whether at the hands of prostate cancer, leukemia, coronary failure, or something else, we'll all agree with my good golfing buddy Ron Baldwin: "We'd all trade in the presidency for Pops."

Being a spiritual leader at home is the prescription that cures the ills of a misdirected life, when the "tyranny of the urgent" has mastered our time and energy and killed our most cherished personal alliances. Yet it's not as complicated as it may seem.

It's as simple as the number *one*.

One time a day, do something really special for your kids' mom.

One time a day, invest in her spiritual well-being.

One time a day, catch your kids in the act of doing something good and tell them about it.

One time a day, tuck your kids into bed and pray with them and read or memorize a Bible verse together.

One time a day, get alone with God.

One time a day, sacrifice something personal for something that benefits your family.

One time a day, ask God to reveal to you anything in your own life that doesn't match your expectations for your kids.

One time a day, forgive completely anyone in your home who has hurt you.

One time a day, say, "I'm sorry," and ask forgiveness for damaging a relationship.

One time a day, help make a child's dream come true.

Total time investment: One to two hours a day.

Return on investment: A lifetime of deep, abiding relationships and an eternity to celebrate.

"All these were descendants of Asher—heads of families, choice men, brave warriors and outstanding leaders" (1 Chronicles 7:40). These priceless words from Old Testament Scripture point to life's greatest adventure, a dad's highest calling, and a home's greatest gift.

The heart of the Tin Man, the courage of the Lion, and the wisdom of the Scarecrow will be yours in abundance as God gives you strength to fulfill your battle cry: "There's no place like home!"

YOUR CHALLENGE

Take another look at the ten "one time a day" actions dads can take as spiritual leaders of their families. Which would be easiest for you to try during the next 24 hours? Are there any you're already doing? Are there any that your spouse or a friend could help you with? Pick one that may stretch you a bit but won't be *too* challenging.

YOUR PLAN

When and how will you take your "one time a day" step? For instance, how might your child respond if you haven't been praying at bedtime and want to start? What could you pray about? How will you explain to your child why this is a good idea? Will you keep track of prayer requests and whether you think they've been answered? Write your ideas in the following space.

While you're at it, consider whether you'd like to make some or all of the ten actions once-a-day commitments. If it sounds too daunting to take on all ten, choose your three favorites and write them here, too.

_____

_____

_____

_____

_____

_____

■ ■ ■

Joe White is president of Kanakuk Kamps and founder of Men at the Cross. He is also the author of more than twenty books and speaks across the country for Men at the Cross, After Dark, Pure Excitement, NFL chapels, and Focus on the Family radio. Joe and his wife, Debbie-Jo, are the parents of four grown children and grandparents of eleven.

No Experience Required

BY JIM DALY

If I close my eyes, I can still see the hospital room and feel the excitement of the big moment. It was August 12, 2000, a brilliantly sunny and warm day in Colorado Springs, our hometown. The excitement and anticipation had been building for months. We were as ready as we'd ever be. At thirty-nine years of age, I was going to be a dad—and I couldn't wait!

After Jean gave birth to Trent and the little guy was placed into my arms, almost everything changed for me.

Everything, that is, except my dysfunctional past.

The arrival of your first child is a reflective season of life. There's the sheer wonder of it all, of course, but many parents tend to wander back in memory to their own childhood. I was no different. In those early days, I found myself looking back and trying to glean some insight from my tumultuous days as a kid.

My father had walked out on us when I was five; my mother died of cancer when I was nine. My stepfather abandoned me on the afternoon of my mother's funeral. When I briefly reunited with my biological dad some time later, he just couldn't resist or break the bad habit of the bottle. He died tragically of exposure when I was twelve.

Jean Stephens and I were married in 1986. Life was great. I was climbing the corporate ladder at International Paper.

But change was in the air. On the verge of another promotion, I received an invitation to work for Focus on the Family—at about half the salary I was making. It made no sense, but the Lord made His will loud and clear. I joined the ministry in 1989, and for the past decade had been devoting my life to leading both the marketing and international divisions.

The assignment was fun and fulfilling, and one that came with a fringe benefit: When you work at a family-help organization, you're going to pick up great parenting advice. I listened every day to the radio broadcast, hosted by Focus's founder, child psychologist Dr. James Dobson. I was soaking up the counsel like a sponge.

Familiarity with parenting advice is encouraging, but you also can know too much. I'll explain. Having immersed myself in marriage and parenting research, I was keenly aware that an extremely high percentage (97 percent) of adults wind up parenting as they were parented. This is good news if you hail from the Ward Cleaver or Cliff Huxtable clans, but bad news if you're a foster kid from Southern California.

It's always been difficult to land a job for which you have no experience. For some reason, fatherhood is exempt from that level of scrutiny. Even the most woefully unqualified are eligible, and millions of guys are hired for the job every year. The screening process isn't very tight.

At the same time, fatherhood is not like operating heavy equipment or flying a jumbo jet (I know, it's far more difficult). Dads receive on-the-job training, and make a ton of mistakes in the process.

Somehow, someway, you (and your son or daughter) find your way through it. If you have the benefit of coming from a solid and stable family, the lessons you learned there are invaluable. But what if you're like me and don't have a reservoir from which to pull good advice?

Here are a few practical suggestions on how to overcome your parenting deficit:

1. *Listen.* God gives us a heart for our kids' hearts. Become a student of your son or daughter by simply listening to not only what he or she is telling you, but how it's being said.

2. *Think.* If you want to know what your child really wants, just recall your own childhood. What did you want? Despite generational differences, children the world over don't want *stuff*—they want *you*. The best things in life are free. Be generous with hugs, kisses, affirmation, and praise. Lift your kids up and tell them how proud you are of them.

3. *Pray.* Never underestimate the power of praying for your children. Pray for and with them at meals, during your commute to work, when dropping them off at school, and quietly in their room while they're sleeping. Let God know that you see them as a blessing.

When I'm old and gray and the boys are grown and gone, the memories of that happy laughter and this innocent era will echo in my mind.

Will I look back with a sense of peace and joy? Or will I have regrets and wonder what could have been? It strikes me that the key to living a regret-free life is often found in one's ability to see the end at the beginning.

When our house becomes quiet and tidy, and the curtain falls on my job of intense, day-to-day parenting, what will I remember about this time? If you're a father, what will you recall? Here are some things I'll remember . . .

Hearing their first cries and holding Trent and Troy tight, scared to death that I would drop them, but knowing I never would . . .

Late-night drives around a dark neighborhood to soothe a colicky baby . . .

First steps, first words, and last-minute, midnight toy assembly jobs on Christmas Eve . . .

The pain of leaving on long ministry trips to faraway places, and the joy of reunions at airports . . .

Vacations on a tight budget—tents that were cold and wet, cars and trailers that wouldn't run, and kids who wouldn't stop . . .

Skinned knees, bloody noses, and a cell phone call about a DVD player that had "smoke but no fire" . . .

Teaching them how to fish . . .

Jumping on the trampoline, riding bikes, playing tag in a dark house . . .

Ballgames and board games . . .

And, best of all, seeing their eyes light up and their hearts open up to the reality of the gospel and the life and resurrection of Jesus Christ.

These are only a smattering of the memories that time won't scatter—because, in the end, these are among the few things that will really matter. You can make fond memories, too—whether or not your own childhood recollections are happy ones.

 ## YOUR CHALLENGE

Fathers who fall short are nothing new. But there seem to be more of them than ever. In the U.S., much has been made of the federal deficit, and for good reason. But the "Daddy Deficit" is far worse and more dangerous.

Children today are craving the attention and affirmation of their fathers. Jim Downing of the Navigators said that the one thing every person wants, regardless of age, is the acceptance and approval of his or her father.

Here is your challenge: Break the cycle! If you grew up in a dysfunctional home, you can, with the Lord's help, be the dad you didn't have but so desperately wanted. It will take work, sacrifice, and prayer, but your son or daughter is well worth the effort.

Regardless of your upbringing, your child needs you to listen to good advice, think back to your own childhood needs, and pray for him or her. Pick one of these to practice during the next 24 hours.

YOUR PLAN

Depending on which of the three suggestions you chose, follow through with one of these action steps.

1. *Listen:* Where do you go for fathering advice? During the next 24 hours, spend at least half an hour reading Bible passages about fathers or parents in general (use a concordance to find them), or reading fatherhood articles at fathers.com or focusonthefamily.com. Use the following space to jot down what you learn.

2. *Think:* Spend at least half an hour remembering what it was like to be the ages your children are now. What did you need most from your father? What did you most want your father to understand about you? If your younger self could time-travel to the present, what would he want to tell you about fathering? Write your answers in the following space.

3. *Pray:* Make a list of two prayer requests about your child's needs, two about your needs as a father, two things about your child for which you're thankful, and two things to thank God for about being a dad. Then spend at least ten minutes talking honestly to God about these concerns and praises.

_____

_____

_____

_____

_____

_____

_____

■ ■ ■

JIM DALY is president and chief executive officer of Focus on the Family. His books include *Finding Home* and *Stronger*, and he serves as co-host of the daily Focus radio broadcast. After earning a bachelor's degree in business administration at California State University, San Bernardino, he went on to work as sales manager at International Paper. He also holds an MBA degree in International Business from Regis University. Jim and his wife, Jean, have two sons.

For more help in taking today's challenge, scan the symbol with your smartphone. See instructions on page xi in the front of this book. Or visit http://www.21DayDadChallenge.com/Day6.

"I'M SORRY, I WAS WRONG!"

BY GRACIA BURNHAM

My three children don't have a father anymore. He died in a gun battle between militant Muslims and Philippine army troops in the Philippine jungle.

Our children were born in the Philippines. Their father—my husband—Martin, was a jungle pilot for New Tribes Mission. Our job was challenging: to provide flight service for tribal missionaries living in remote villages. We flew food, medicine, and cargo to their tribal stations and served as an air ambulance during medical emergencies.

Martin loved what he did. Our family worked together to "get the job done." Our children were given simple tasks to perform in the hangar. We loved our life overseas.

In 2001, Martin and I left our children with co-workers at our flight base and traveled to the southern Philippines to do some flying. In the wrong place at the wrong time, we were taken hostage by a group of Muslim extremists. For more than a year we lived in the jungle, prisoners of terrorists. We moved constantly to avoid the Philippine soldiers who were trying to rescue us. We slept on the jungle floor and bathed in streams and rivers. We went hungry and witnessed the atrocities that these men committed against other captives and unsuspecting villagers.

One day I was bemoaning our fate out loud. I asked Martin, "If you could go back and change anything, what would you change?"

His answer surprised me. I expected him to say he would change the circumstances that led up to our being held captive. What he said was, "I would change the time that I spoke harshly to Mindy, or I would change the time when I was too busy to go outside and 'toss the pigskin' with the boys. Those are the things I would change."

I learned a lesson that day. When life takes an awful turn, you won't be concerned about your career, your possessions, or your position in life. As a dad, you'll be concerned about your children.

That's what Martin talked about all the time in the jungle. "I wonder how the kids are doing?" And, "It's Friday night. Maybe the kids are watching the Rose Hill Rockets play football." (We'd learned that our children had been sent back to the United States to live with their grandparents in Kansas. What we couldn't know is that Jeff had *become* a Rose Hill Rocket and was playing football on Friday nights.)

How we missed our kids!

Martin taught me a good many things in the jungle:

1. How to tie a knot to keep a hammock cord secure around a tree.
2. Lie flat on the ground in a gun battle so you make the smallest target possible until someone tells you what to do.
3. See yourself for what you really are.

That last lesson wasn't a comfortable one. Up until our captivity, I'd thought of myself as a pretty good person. After all, we'd left the American dream to help others, hadn't we? In the jungle, I began seeing things in me that were shocking—hatred, envy, bitterness.

As I look back, I see that I was filled with spiritual pride. In our house, I was the pusher. I wanted our family to look and be perfect, and I was going to be the one who pushed to make that happen. Martin was the one full of grace, and now *he* was saying to *me*, "If I could do it all over again, I would apologize to the kids for being so hard on them."

I took that lesson to heart! After Martin died in the gun battle that rescued me, I came home determined to give grace to our children instead of finding fault with them. I think they have seen the difference.

Doing that without Martin hasn't been easy. Single parenting presents challenges. God can do anything, though, and when we lean on Him those challenges are overcome.

Maybe you have challenges, too. Are you a single dad? Have you lost a spouse? Did you grow up without a father's positive influence?

Perhaps it would help to do what I do: Think of young Timothy in the Scriptures. No mention is made of his father when Paul, his mentor, writes him letters. Paul encourages Timothy to keep the faith that his mother and grandmother instilled in him. We don't know that whole story, but Timothy was greatly used in the early church. Paul calls him a "man of God" in 1 Timothy 6:11.

Often I've told my children, "Let's not use the fact that you don't have a dad anymore as an excuse. Scripture promises that we have been given everything we need to live a godly life (2 Peter 1:3), so let's let God use us regardless of our circumstances." God has been good to us—grace upon grace!

These days I am quick to ask my children's forgiveness—even if it means waking one of them up at midnight, as I recently had to do. "Zach," I confessed, "I couldn't get to sleep because I said some really harsh things to you after supper. I should never have talked to you that way. Will you forgive me?" Zach was gracious and forgiving.

Asking forgiveness isn't easy, is it? There are lots of excuses we can make for ourselves:

"But how is he going to learn discipline if I don't teach him?"

"It's my job to see that she behaves. That's what parents are for."

"They don't listen unless I yell."

When I begin to be defensive and make excuses after I've been unfair, I ask myself, "Could I have accomplished the same thing using a kinder, more productive strategy?"

I also ask myself why I expect my kids to be better than I am:

Is my room always clean?

Do I ever leave things undone until the deadline and then scramble to get them done?

Have I ever made a huge mistake or done something with good intentions and it ended disastrously?

Have I ever lied to get myself out of a jam?

I will always be thankful for Martin's example of humility and for the lesson he taught me that day in the jungle. It has affected my parenting. Our kids aren't perfect, but they are good kids.

Zach has his father's laugh. I love hearing it as it floats up from the basement. Mindy has Martin's sense of humor. She makes me laugh like Martin did. Jeff got his dad's piloting skills and flies for a mission organization in Africa. All three kids love the Lord and tell me they love me all the time.

They learned that from their daddy!

YOUR CHALLENGE

Apologize to your child for something hurtful you've done, even if you did it a long time ago. Don't use this time to point out something your child should have done differently; just say you're sorry and why.

YOUR PLAN

Write down what you'll apologize for. Add two things you'd like
your child to take away from that conversation. (Examples: the feeling that he or she is loved; the realization that being a "real man"
doesn't mean never having to say you're sorry.) Then note when and
where you'll have this talk.

_____

_____

_____

_____

_____

_____

_____

■ ■ ■

GRACIA BURNHAM is the founder of the Martin & Gracia Burnham Foundation, which supports missionary aviation, tribal mission work, showing Christ's love to the Muslim community, and
assisting Christians who suffer for their faith. Her books, written
with Dean Merrill, include _In the Presence of My Enemies_ and _To Fly
Again._ Gracia's story has been told in numerous TV specials, and she
speaks frequently at churches, conferences, and schools. She has a
bachelor's degree in Christian education—and three children, all of
whom are now young adults.

Where Seldom Is Heard an Encouraging Word

BY GARY J. OLIVER, PH.D.

When I was a little boy I spent many a Saturday morning watching cowboy shows where I would frequently hear Roy Rogers or Gene Autry sing "Home on the Range." Do you remember the words to the chorus?

> *Home, home on the range*
> *Where the deer and the antelope play;*
> *Where seldom is heard a discouraging word*
> *And the skies are not cloudy all day.*

It's sad to say that many of our homes today aren't like the one on the range. Rather than seldom hearing a discouraging word, many of us live where seldom is heard an *encouraging* word.

It's so easy for us when we're tired and stressed-out to become more negative and critical and only notice what's wrong or what someone has failed to do. A lack of encouragement leads to discouragement—and depression, which is the number one mental health problem of our time.

After close to thirty years of being a dad and teaching marriage and family counseling to many graduate and post-graduate students, I've learned that one of the simplest yet most powerful keys to being an effective dad is to cultivate an encouraging environment for our kids.

Do you remember a time when you were criticized, minimized, or put down? When was the last time you worked hard to do a good job and the only thing that was noticed was what you didn't do or what you did that wasn't good enough? Perhaps your hard work wasn't noticed at all.

What did it feel like? How did you feel about yourself and the person criticizing you? Were you encouraged or discouraged? Were you motivated to do better, or did you want to give up?

An encouraging environment is one in which our kids know they're of value to God and to us. It's one in which we spend more time building them up than we do scolding and correcting them. It's one in which we honor them by speaking respectfully to them and looking for signs that they're growing in Christlike character.

An encouraging environment is one where we emphasize catching our kids doing good rather than catching them making mistakes. It's one where we invest more energy in praising them for even small steps in the right direction than in criticizing them for falling short of our expectations.

This simple activity is so easy to forget. When I was a young father I criticized one of my boys for not making his bed. I didn't yell or anything like that, but he knew that I was disappointed. Early the next week my wife said, "Gary, several days ago you criticized Andrew for not making his bed—but he has made it every day since then. Have you noticed it and praised him for following through?"

I'm embarrassed to say that my answer was no. But within minutes I went to him, acknowledged his hard work, and told him how much I appreciated it. His smile let me know I had encouraged him.

An encouraging environment is one in which we respond to our children's pleasant as well as painful emotions. Without intending to, many of us primarily react to our children (or our spouses) when our emotions are inappropriate or out of control. What many kids learn is that if they want attention, the only way they'll get it is by being in a crisis or creating one.

An encouraging environment is one where it's safe for any family member to make mistakes. In fact, it's not only safe but provides a place where kids begin to learn that God can actually use our failures to help us grow. They learn that Romans 8:28 is really true, that God works in all things "for the good of those who love him." They also learn the truth of 2 Corinthians 12:9-10—that with God's help when we are weak we can be strong. They learn that one of the best questions to ask after making a mistake is "What can I learn from this?" and not "How can I hide this so I won't get in trouble?"

How can you begin to create an environment like that in your home?

Get out a pad and pencil and write down the names of your kids. Now ask yourself the following questions and write your responses under each child's name.

What are this child's strengths?
What does this child do well?
What says "love" to this child?
What makes this child laugh?
What gives this child joy?
What is it about this child that I'm thankful for?
What are three good things this child has done in the past week?

Then ask yourself another set of questions:

How many times during the last week have I given this child a specific compliment or thanked him or her for something positive?

When is the last time I "caught" this child being kind or exhibiting the fruit of the Spirit or asking for forgiveness, and let him or her know how much I appreciated it?

When is the last time I gave this child an inexpensive gift just for the fun of it?

When is the last time I let this child know he or she is precious in my sight and in God's?

In Romans 15:5 God is described as one who gives endurance and encouragement. In 1 Thessalonians 5:11 and Hebrews 3:13, we're told to encourage one another. In Acts 4:36 we meet a disciple named Joseph from the island of Cyprus—whom everyone knew by his nickname, Barnabas, which means "son of encouragement."

As a father, what might your nickname be? I don't know about you, but I'd love to be known by my boys as a "father of encouragement."

Here's how simple this can be. Several years ago when my son Andrew was five, I went into his room as I did almost every night to chat and pray with him. One evening I decided to make up a song about all the things I appreciated about him and started singing. The words didn't rhyme, the tune changed with every new verse, and my voice didn't sound that good.

After a couple of minutes I ran out of things to sing. As I started to pray with him Andrew interrupted, looked up at me, squeezed my hand, and said, "Sing to me some more, Daddy, sing to me some more."

He loved to hear me share what I liked and appreciated about him. And that's the only time in my life someone has asked me to keep on singing.

YOUR CHALLENGE

Set aside a couple of minutes today to specifically build up each of your kids. At first they may not notice, but after a few days of doing this you'll discover the power of an encouraging word.

YOUR PLAN

Use the following space to answer the two sets of questions in this chapter. Examples: *What says "love" to this child? When is the last time I let this child know he or she is precious in my sight and in God's?*

Then jot down a few ideas for encouraging statements you can make and when you'll make them.

_____

_____

_____

_____

_____

■ ■ ■

GARY J. OLIVER, TH.M., PH.D., is executive director of The Center for Relationship Enrichment and professor of psychology and practical theology at John Brown University in Siloam Springs, Arkansas. He is also the author of more than twenty books including *Raising Sons and Loving It!*

Unforgettable

BY CLARK HUNT

There are dates we fathers need to remember, and dates we'll never forget.

With meetings and appointments, business lunches and deadlines, soccer practices and parent-teacher conferences, the dates we need to remember can quickly fill up our calendars—leaving little free time for the things that are most important.

Then there are the dates we'll never forget. For me that includes December 19, 1992, the day my beautiful wife, Tavia, agreed to marry me—and October 23, 1993, when she actually went through with it. I will never forget my mother's birthday in March or the date in mid-December when my dad went to be with the Lord.

But perhaps the most unforgettable date on my calendar is March 29. On that day in 1999 Tavia and I were blessed with our first child, Grace. Much to our surprise and joy, we welcomed our third child, Ava, on the same date seven years later. (Our son Knobel, ever the individual, decided July was best for his debut.)

Sharing a birthday can be challenging for a child, and Tavia does a wonderful job finding creative ways to make both Grace and Ava feel celebrated on their shared special day. Several years ago we tried a joint birthday party for the girls at our home; Grace was content to split the attention with toddler Ava, who was indifferent to the focus of the party provided she could open presents and eat cake and ice cream.

It was a fun party, one that Tavia and I remember fondly. But in the years since, we've made a point to celebrate their birth days separately. While Grace and Ava are sisters who share a birth date and enjoy celebrating together, they are two unique people of different ages, interests, and preferences. They express and receive love in their own ways, and they face different challenges at school and with their friends.

Because no two kids are alike, they can't be raised as a set. They deserve one-on-one time with their dad—time that's scheduled and protected from all that competition on our calendars.

Children become more distinct as they grow up, and seeing my kids develop their own unique personalities is one of my favorite aspects of being a parent. When I witness Ava learning to be a good teammate on the soccer field, or watch as Knobel summons his courage to tell a joke and gets a laugh from a room full of strangers, it brings me great joy to see them mature.

In the same way, Tavia and I are witnessing Grace's transition from a child to a teenager almost overnight. The little girl who loved to catch lizards in the backyard or kick the soccer ball around with Dad after work has become the young woman interested in fashion and friends—some of whom are boys, much to my chagrin. When I began to notice that these changes further enriched the strong bond between mother and daughter, it made me concerned that I would soon find myself on the outside looking in with Grace.

We still spent a considerable amount of time together as a family, and I would always ask Grace about her day at dinnertime, but I still feared that we might drift apart. It soon became apparent to me that I needed to go the extra step to develop my relationship with her.

One day it occurred to me that the best way to strengthen that relationship would be to set aside time on a regular basis for just the two of us. We call these times "Dad Dates."

My primary goal on "Dad Dates" is to spend one-on-one time with Grace and grow our relationship. But I also want to demonstrate to her how she should expect to be treated by her future husband. As a result, each time I take intentional steps to model the qualities a Christian man should display.

The formula for remembering and making the most of this individual time is simple:

1. *Schedule a time in advance.* Setting aside time with Grace on my calendar is critical for me. I am always surprised at how easy it is to get distracted by other commitments if I don't carve out specific time in my schedule. It also shows Grace that her time is valuable and should be respected, while giving her something fun to look forward to during the week.

2. *Have a plan.* Whether we're attending a basketball game, venturing to an amusement park, or just going out to eat, I always try to have a plan for our time together. I find that it helps me relax and focus on the time with Grace. I want to communicate to her that a man should be thoughtful and creative.

3. *Set the standard.* Young women today are inundated with misleading messages about how they should look, how they should dress, how they should act, and, most disheartening to a father, what *they* have to do to get a man. We have a small window as fathers to teach our daughters how they should expect to be treated by young men. On our dates I try to focus on the simple things that communicate respect—don't be late, dress appropriately, compliment her, open the door, etc.

4. *Listen.* I've found that no matter what the activity, Grace's favorite part of our time together is having my undivided attention. Though I generally feel I have a pretty good understanding of what's going on in my daughter's life, I am always surprised by what I learn on our dates. Her willingness to open up and share what's going on in her life only increases the more we spend one-on-one time together.

As a man, a husband, a father, a provider, and a believer, it is a daily challenge for me to find balance in my life. All too often I find myself at the end of the day long on intentions and short on time. Our time is valuable because it's limited—and not guaranteed.

Spending quality, one-on-one time with my daughter reinforces our bond and brings me great joy. But I hope it also provides Grace with a road map for her future relationships. As Proverbs 22:6 suggests, kids remember these things: "Train a child in the way he should go, and when he is old he will not turn from it."

Just a couple of months ago, we celebrated Grace's twelfth birthday with a group of her friends—her last until becoming a teenager. Before I know it, though I hope several years from now, she will come asking for my permission to go on her first date. When it does happen, I'm sure I'll remind her of the lessons from our "Dad Dates" she needs to remember.

They just so happen to be some of the same dates I will never forget.

YOUR CHALLENGE

Is spending one-on-one time with your children a priority? If you have more than one child, what are some of their differences as well as their similarities? How has each child been changing lately? Do you feel connected or out of touch?

During the next 24 hours, schedule at least thirty minutes with each of your kids. If you're already booked up, make the appointments today for the next available opportunity. Check your child's schedule to make sure you aren't competing with a football practice, favorite TV show, play date, or youth group activity.

Don't keep this appointment a secret. Write it on the family calendar. Announce it at the dinner table. You might even consider giving each child a formal invitation that you've created on the computer or by hand, if you think that's something he or she would enjoy.

YOUR PLAN

These steps for "Dad Dates" are simple and work for both girls and boys: Schedule a time in advance, have a plan, set the standard, and listen. For this "first date," make it a priority to learn what each child enjoys doing right now, and what he or she would like to do during your one-on-one times. Do this in a setting in which he or she is likely to relax—the swings at the park, the mall food court, the hammock in the backyard. In the following space, write notes for future reference on what you discover during your conversation.

_____

_____

_____

_____

_____

_____

■ ■ ■

CLARK HUNT is chairman of the board and chief executive officer of the Kansas City Chiefs. He is also a founding investor-operator in Major League Soccer and chairman of Hunt Sports Group, which oversees two Major League Soccer franchises—FC Dallas and the Columbus Crew—and has been in the forefront of stadium development in the United States. He holds a degree in business administration from Southern Methodist University and serves on the SMU board of trustees. He and his wife, Tavia, have three children.

What's in a Name

BY SHAUN ALEXANDER

I could see that, for this season of my life, every morning was going to start out the same. I would get up, say my prayers, read my Bible, and head to the kitchen to cook my little girls breakfast. A bit different from heading to football practice or morning workouts, I must say.

My wife had just given birth to our fourth child—my first son—and I was excited. "I love this li'l man of God!" I declared.

So with three little girls (ages two, three, and five) all smiles and ready to roll every morning, I embraced the routine. It became a joy and honor to fix breakfast, have talks, and plan the first part of the day—the one called, "Eat, pray, and play until Mommy gets up."

One morning I was making one of our family breakfast specialties—Fruit Explosion Oatmeal. (In our house, oatmeal runs neck and neck with pancakes.) Seeing my three princesses chowing down on their breakfast was always a delight.

As I watched them eat, with their heads practically in the bowl, I noticed that my two-year-old had oatmeal on the side of her face. Without making a big deal of it, I said, "Hey, Beautiful, you have oatmeal on your cheek."

To my surprise, in unison and without hesitation, all three of the girls looked up. Then all three grabbed their napkins and wiped their faces!

I laugh with joy every time I think about this story. Do I have three vain daughters? Of course not. The simple fact is that since the time they were born, I gave them a name—even more, an *identity.* From birth my princesses have been told they are beautiful, loved, and valuable.

That identity will be hard for them to ever stop believing. Not that I would want them to.

Proverbs 18:21 says, "The tongue has the power of life and death." Every word you say has power. That's especially true of names. Use them to mark your child—in a good way.

When it comes to names, I think of my father. He called me "Champ" more than he called me Shaun.

Nobody could ever tell me I wasn't a winner. I was a champion! I was told that from birth. Even when my parents divorced, every phone call started with, "Hey, Champ." My father made mistakes at times, but one thing he did right was to help define my identity.

Names you call your child will leave a mark. Choose them carefully. Your kids will hold on to whatever names you give them.

That happens whether the names are positive or negative. When I was a teenager, I knew a girl who bragged about how carefree—and careless—she was. I was amazed to hear her tell stories week after week about drink after drink and guy after guy. It went from shocking to sad as the year went by.

She was a beautiful girl; I couldn't understand why she lived that way.

One day I decided that after school I would find out. As I looked her in the face to ask a simple "Why?" she began to cry. She was getting ready to open up, I could tell.

That's when her dad drove up to take her home. He honked the car horn three times.

"Hey, Party Girl," he shouted through the open window. "Let's ride!"

That's when I knew: Her father had given her the wrong name.

Dad, if you tell her she is a prize, she will act like it. Especially if *you* act like she is one, too.

And remember: If you don't give them names, somebody else will.

Consider the father who never gave his son a name. The dad looks at his son with shock and disappointment. "So you stole the stuff from the store, drank at your friend's house, cheated on the girl of your dreams with some stranger at a party, and you went to the place you know you should never go. Why?"

The son looks at his father. "They call me Never Scared," he says. "I'm the Ice Man. I'll do the things that others are scared to do."

Later, the dad cries. He knows he has let some teens give his son an identity. He's allowed the unmolded to mold his son.

This is called the blind leading the blind.

I believe that nobody wants to be known as a drunkard, sexually promiscuous, a drug user, a club fighter, or a bar hopper. But I also believe a person—especially a male—will do anything to get an identity.

You better name your child before someone else does.

That takes a little time and effort, though, more than many fathers spend with their children. If your time is limited, make sure you're using some of it to give your child an identity. Even if you have to spend some of the time correcting or disciplining, try to start and end it identifying your child in a positive way. A child who knows you think he or she is great will stand much taller and stronger when hard times come.

Give your kids an identity and they'll grab it. That identity will become their stance, their way to approach life. It will become the fuel for their confidence. With confidence your child will have a greater ability to make his or her own decisions.

That leads to setting healthy boundaries. Children with strong, positive identities decide for themselves what they will and won't do, what they like and don't like. That helps cultivate self-respect, which kills most forms of peer pressure and creates focus, direction, and clarity.

The result: a child of *substance*. A child of substance usually finds success—and even more importantly, significance.

Want children of substance? Start by naming them thoughtfully and giving them the identities they need. Then nourish those identities by maintaining a loving relationship.

So how do you do that in the middle of everyday life's busyness?

At our house we try to remember that great relationships aren't built of laws or rigid rules, but of vulnerable communication, honesty, healthy conflicts, order, and direction. We have some things we try to do daily, weekly, and monthly to nurture those qualities. The activities themselves aren't the goal. The goal is to love on our kids, teach them, mold them, and release them to be whatever God has called them to be.

Here's an example—the end of a typical day at our house. After the kids take baths, brush teeth, and put on pajamas, we sit in a room together and ask two questions:

- What was your favorite part of the day?
- Who or what are you thankful for today?

The answers let us know what's on our children's hearts and minds.

Then there's a typical week at our house. I have a one-on-one conversation with each child, each week. The child's needs and my schedule determine the when, where, and how long of this "convo." During these conversations I make sure to tell my kids I love them; you can never say "I love you" enough, but make sure you say it on that day. I also affirm them; I love telling them about the good I see in them.

Finally, there's our typical month. Once a month, one-on-one, the girls and I go out and hang. Sometimes it's eating, sometimes it's shopping—even if we don't buy anything. Sometimes it's going to a park, sometimes it's going to a bookstore. I call it Daddy Dates. Their purpose: To let my children know that I'll stop my world to be with them.

We do these things so that I can mark my kids with love. I want them to know who they are in Christ and that they're fearfully and wonderfully made.

Not long after my firstborn son turned two, he was running down the hallway when he tripped and fell—hard.

"You all right, Man of God?" I called.

"Yes," he said without hesitation.

I smiled. *He knows his name!* I thought. *I'm giving him his identity.*

Have we missed some opportunities to build our kids' identities? Of course—but we've made some imprints, too.

I hope you'll go and do the same today.

YOUR CHALLENGE

Give your child a positive nickname. Make sure it's one that he or she likes. Choose one that points your child toward the person you want him or her to be (Man of God, CEO, VP, etc.). It should let your child know you think highly of him or her (Princess, Handsome, Champ). You might want to use one that reminds you of a special time you had together (Philly, for example, if you had a great vacation there). You may have to try a few until something sticks.

YOUR PLAN

During the next 24 hours, call your child by a positive nickname instead of his or her real name. If your child doesn't object, try to do that every day for one week.

Use the following space to brainstorm nicknames you might use. Then, if you're married, ask your wife to help you pick the one you'll try first.

_____

_____

_____

_____

_____

■ ■ ■

SHAUN ALEXANDER is the award-winning author of *Touchdown Alexander* and his newest book, *The Walk*. After attending the University of Alabama, Shaun was drafted in the first round by the Seattle Seahawks. A three-time Pro Bowl selection, he set an NFL touchdown record (28) in 2005 and became the first Seahawk to win the MVP of the NFL. He led his team to the Super Bowl the same year. Shaun now partners with a number of organizations and travels with his family sharing the message of Jesus, family, and community.

For more help in taking today's challenge, scan the symbol with your smartphone. See instructions on page xi in the front of this book. Or visit http://www.21DayDadChallenge.com/Day10.

The Forever Stamp

BY MARK DEMOSS

When my first child, Georgia, was sixteen years old, she had what seemed to have been a tough day. That evening I went to kiss her good night. I found her on her bed, leafing through a box of papers.

"What's that?" I asked.

"It's my letterbox," she replied.

I hadn't known she had a letterbox. But when I looked over her shoulder, I saw one of my letters to her—and smiled.

I'm a big letter-writer. I'm also part of a very small minority, according to numerous studies of such things.

Letter writing is a lost art, and I believe family relationships have suffered as a result. Cheap long-distance telephone service, universal availability of cell phones, and the ease of text messaging and e-mail have all contributed to the demise of the old-fashioned letter. What a shame!

I still cherish a letter my father wrote me when I was seventeen—more than thirty years ago. I was away for the summer selling books door-to-door, something he'd encouraged me to do for all the valuable lessons I would learn. It was the toughest thing I've ever done, but his letter lifted my spirits. More than that, it reminded me how proud he was of me, how much he loved me. I already knew that, but I sure loved reading it on his letterhead.

That was the last letter I ever received from my father. Less than three months later he was in heaven—just fifty-three years old. As I approach fifty, I still pull that letter out of its file and reread it.

I wonder: Thirty years from now, will anyone be pulling up an e-mail or text message he or she received today? Will our children ever sit on their beds scrolling through a special "letter inbox" on their smart phones, looking for comfort after a difficult day at school?

Georgia got married recently. I placed a letter on her bed the night before her wedding. I suspect she'll read this letter many times in the years ahead. Letters can become history books for a family, journals chronicling special memories, milestones, challenges, and victories. They remind us where we were and what we were doing at crucial times during our lives together. One day they'll be tangible reminders of the people we love who've gone on to heaven.

I frequently write letters to all my children (and to my wife). How could we possibly write too much? Consequently, my kids are learning to be letter-writers—which is even more rare in their age group. The number of obvious occasions for a letter is infinite: a birthday (forget the e-card, okay?), a big ballgame or tennis match, a breakup with a boyfriend or girlfriend, a school award, a concert performance, a good (or bad) report card, getting a driver's license, graduating from anything—or even for no obvious reason at all.

The impact of a letter always exceeds the effort it took to write it. Always. Some notes or letters can be written in just five minutes but positively affect the recipient for days or months—even years.

You can increase the impact by investing in a stamp, too. Usually I take to my office a letter I've addressed to one of our three children and mail it back to our home. I could much more easily walk upstairs and put the letter on the recipient's bed, but practically everyone likes to get mail. So go ahead and buy a roll of stamps for the benefit of your relationship with your children.

I once found a short note I'd written to Madison, our youngest, taped to her bathroom mirror. It contained a Scripture verse I wanted to bless her with, and apparently it was doing just that every time she stood in front of her mirror. Is that worth five minutes of time and a "forever" stamp? Madison often teases me about mailing a letter to someone in the same house, but I know she appreciates it.

Between our two girls we have a son named Mookie. Much of my life with him has involved the sport of golf, which he's now playing in college. I've written him after so many tournaments, regardless of his score. I always tell him how proud I am of him and how hard he's working, and commend him for how he conducted himself on the course. His grandfather is a big letter-writer as well, and Mookie keeps all his letters.

I've written each of our children a special letter as he or she began the final year of high school, and another letter upon graduation. With the graduation letter I gave each one a Bible I'd used in my personal devotions for at least several years, leaving the pages full of my notes and underlining.

Mookie got the Bible I'd used the longest; I'd probably read through it fifteen times. He then wrote me a letter on his graduation day, thanking me for my letters and for always telling him how proud I was of him. He noted that he didn't always like hearing it right after tournaments where he didn't play that well, but that he appreciated it nonetheless. He then added a P.S. I'll remember the rest of my life: "By the way, I've been reading Proverbs every day since eighth grade because of you."

When my daughter Georgia's fiancé came to ask for our blessing to marry her, I gave him a special gift (since girls get an engagement ring but most guys get nothing), along with a letter. While the letter clearly blessed him, I really wrote it knowing how much it would bless *her*—which indeed it did when he read it to her after he proposed to her on Christmas Eve.

None of these letters has taken me long to write. Yet every one of them will have a long-lasting impact on my children. My wife, April, and I have even written letters to our children which they won't see until our deaths. We want them to have another reminder of our love for them and of some of the things we value most.

I know they'll keep that letter—forever.

YOUR CHALLENGE

Will you commit to writing to your children periodically, for any reason or no particular reason at all? If you've depended on e-mail or texting, resist that habit and write some letters. See if your kids don't create their own letterboxes.

You only need five or ten minutes to get started. Begin by writing your children today. Get some note cards and letterhead of different types and sizes so they don't all look the same. Buy a supply of "forever" stamps from the Postal Service, which lock in the current postage rate. Then sit back and watch your blessings pass on to your children.

YOUR PLAN

In the following space, make some notes about the letters you'll write today. Are congratulations in order for your child? Have you seen him or her make spiritual progress in the last year? Or is he or she struggling in school, missing a friend, fearing an upcoming test or medical procedure? Is there a milestone in the recent past or near future? Does he or she most need a lift, a pat on the back, or a challenge?

_____

_____

_____

_____

_____

_____

_____

_____

■ ■ ■

MARK DeMoss founded The DeMoss Group in 1991, where he has served some of the world's most prominent Christian organizations—shaping events and campaigns as well as providing public relations counsel and strategic planning. He is the author of *The Little Red Book of Wisdom*. Mark and his wife, April, live in Atlanta, Georgia, and have three children.

Buy a Unicycle

BY JAY PAYLEITNER

It's okay that no one has ever ridden the unicycle hanging from the ceiling in our garage. Really, it is.

We bought it for my son Randy's ninth birthday for about seventy-five bucks. He gave it a try, spending a total of maybe six or eight hours goofing with it. His brothers and sister also spent varying amounts of time experimenting with the one-wheeled contraption. Isaac probably stayed up the longest—eight or ten seconds. None of them ever really got the hang of it.

I'm absolutely sure that out of my five children, one or two had the physical agility and mental acuity to become an expert unicyclist. It would have taken hours of practice, perhaps an entire summer. I certainly am not going to blame any of my kids for not following through. The mental gyroscope required for mastering the unicycle cannot be detected by visual inspection. Plus, I don't think any of them ever caught the vision of how cool it would be to ride down the street on one wheel.

Maybe each of them did a cost-benefit analysis of the time it would take, the amount of frustration he or she might endure, Dad's expectations, the reality that it might not even be possible, and the immediate and long-term usefulness of having that particular skill. For whatever reason, each of them chose not to go for it. Instead, they played catch, swam, rode two-wheeled bikes, climbed trees, invented backyard games, watched the Cubs lose on WGN, tormented their siblings, hung out with friends, and maybe even read a book or two.

In the meantime, the unicycle got pulled out of the garage every once in a while. A garage-exploring neighbor boy would see it and want to give it a try. One or two kids from down the street claimed to be experts, but failed to impress. Now it hangs from the ceiling, just low enough that I bump my head on it once or twice each season.

So, was Randy's birthday gift a waste of money? I don't think so. As part of our annual child-rearing budget, $75 is a drop in the bucket. The U.S. Department of Agriculture recently calculated that the average cost for a two-parent, middle-income family to raise a kid to age eighteen is $221,190—and that doesn't include college. No wonder I'm broke.

What that unicycle in my garage really represents is one of the many doors this dad has opened for his children.

That's one of our most important jobs; dads open doors. We place new opportunities in front of our kids, do a little song-and-dance sell job, and then get out of the way. We can instruct them, but we can't do it for them. We can sign them up and even make them give it a try, but we can't flip that little switch in their brain that says, "I have found my life's passion." We can spark a vision, but we shouldn't try to live vicariously through them.

You know what I'm talking about. If you wrestled in high school, you may choose to install a regulation wrestling mat in your basement, but you already know that sport isn't for everyone. You can buy a baby grand piano, but that doesn't mean your child is going to be the next Franz Liszt or Billy Joel. You can set up an art easel in the corner of your rec room, but its primary use may be as a giant sketchpad holder for Pictionary.

Does that mean you've failed as a father? Of course not. As a matter of fact, the wrestling mat, piano, and easel may actually be a catalyst for some unexpected activity that *does* bring a new vision to your son's or daughter's life. Somersaulting on that mat—not wrestling—may lead to a career as a world-class gymnast. The kid who lives down the street may drop by and noodle on that piano, motivating your daughter to discover her passion as a jazz vocalist. As emcee for those rec room party games, your son may polish his skills and find his niche as a game show host or motivational speaker.

Only God knows how those life pieces fit together. As fathers, we're called to keep opening doors of opportunity and experience for our children. Some will slam closed; many will remain open for years and then gently swing shut. Still others will lead to real-life laboratories, auditoriums, classrooms, boardrooms, gymnasiums, and galleries. As our children peek, sneak, walk, and dance through those doorways, they are learning who they are in God's eyes.

You probably know the oft-quoted proverb for parents, "Train a child in the way he should go, and when he is old he will not turn from it" (Proverbs 22:6). Bible scholars pluck several truths from that sentence. The verse reminds parents of our God-given responsibility, confirms that children need to be led intentionally, and verifies that lessons learned early have staying power. Some translators believe "in the way he should go" means "according to his bent." If that's the case, it's our job to introduce our children to a wide variety of activities so they can assess their abilities and test their skills. That's how they find "the way they should go."

Fathers are especially good at challenging our kids to try new things. While moms tend to like "safe," dads often like "adventure." When the young skateboarder skins his knee, Mom runs for the peroxide and Band-Aid, but Dad knows the fallen rider needs to get back on the board. When Mom peruses a park district brochure, she probably looks for activities at which her child has already enjoyed a hint of success. Dads may look for options not yet attempted: archery, spelunking, rappelling, kayaking.

What moms don't realize is that dads usually know what we're doing when we push our kids to the edge of their comfort zone. We want to be there to take pride in their newfound success, but we also stay poised to spring quickly into rescue mode if they need help. We know they're going to fall off that unicycle. But we also know that short-term setback will occur within the safe haven of our driveway. We're watching, cheering, and ready if and when they need us.

To put it another way, a mother's encouragement takes away the fear of failure—affirming kids have nothing to lose. A father's encouragement creates a vision for victory—affirming kids have everything to win.

There are no regrets from this dad about that $75 purchase—except that I always wanted to ride a unicycle myself. So I guess I'm guilty of seeking a smidgen of personal satisfaction by living vicariously through one of my progeny. But in this case, it didn't get very far.

Still, my recommendation is to "buy a unicycle." No matter what, it'll be okay, dad. Even if your kids just give it a reasonable effort and then choose not to walk through that particular door.

And even if they master the one-wheeled beast and join the circus.

YOUR CHALLENGE

Swing open a new door—athletic, artistic, scholastic, scientific, spiritual, musical, intellectual, or relational. In the next 24 hours, do something to . . .

- Encourage your kids to explore their gifts.
- Make it as painless as possible to try something new.
- Come alongside them.
- Applaud a small victory.
- Laugh with them about a setback or botched attempt—preferably one of your own.
- Move in and out of their world so that when they ask your opinion, you can respond by asking the right questions.
- Help steer them toward a career, hobby, or ministry opportunity God seems to have prepared just for them.

YOUR PLAN

In the following space, write your ideas for doing one of the aforementioned today.

For the longer term, think back to your childhood, especially when you were the age your kids are now. In the space below, brainstorm ten vivid memories of things you did way back then. (Examples: caught tadpoles, picked raspberries, built a go-cart, shot a home movie, carved a decoy, taught yourself harmonica, set up a lemonade stand.) Do one of those things with your son or daughter in the next week.

Or just buy 'em a unicycle![3]

_____

_____

_____

_____

_____

_____

_____

_____

■ ■ ■

JAY PAYLEITNER is a behind-the-scenes veteran of Christian radio serving as producer for *Josh McDowell Radio*, *Jesus Freaks Radio*, *Project Angel Tree* with Chuck Colson, and *Today's Father* for the National Center for Fathering. He's also a popular speaker at men's events and the author of *52 Things Kids Need from a Dad* and *365 Ways to Say "I Love You" to Your Kids*. Jay and his wife, Rita, make their home in the Chicago area, where they've raised five children and cared for ten foster babies. His weekly "dadblog" is found at http://fathers52.com.

You Lead, They Succeed

BY CHIP INGRAM

When I was growing up, my dad wasn't a Christian. He was in the Marines in World War II and wasn't the type to say, "I love you."

But Dad showed me love by instilling in me the importance of setting clear goals, developing a strategy to achieve them, and working like crazy to make them happen. He wanted me to be happy—and from his perspective, success was the key to happiness.

By age twelve I was a workaholic. I had two paper routes plus a lawn business, and had figured out how to lend my parents three thousand dollars at 6 percent interest!

Life was about me, about achieving my dreams that someday would make me happy. But on my high school graduation night, something happened that shocked my values to the core.

A friend smiled at me and innocently said, "Chip, you must be really happy tonight. You've got a basketball scholarship to college, a pretty girlfriend, and you've won lots of awards with a great future ahead of you. How does it feel to be so successful?"

With stunning clarity, I suddenly realized that I felt anything but happy. In spite of achieving many of my personal goals, I felt terribly alone. I'd worked the formula: Set clear goals, develop a strategy, and work like crazy. I'd tried to charm everyone around me to fulfill my desires, only to discover it felt . . . empty.

At that moment I began to wonder: *If I keep going at this pace and set new goals for my career, house, money, and a beautiful wife in the future, what would be the point of it?* This realization would change my life.

By God's grace, I soon began a journey in search of meaning and purpose. Two weeks later at a Fellowship of Christian Athletes camp in central Ohio, I found myself exploring the offer of my heavenly Father through His Son, Jesus Christ. I prayed, "God, if You exist, reveal Yourself to me. If You are real, show me what You want from me."

Opening the Bible for the first time in my adult life, I read, "Offer your bodies as living sacrifices, holy and pleasing to God— this is your spiritual act of worship" (Romans 12:1).

Since then, I've come to grasp that God wants us to know and feel that we are His cherished children living in joyful union with Him. It's not about our performance, but about our relationship with Him. As we journey through experiences in the ups and downs of life, our heavenly Father wants us to live out of the favor and grace that we already possess in our relationship with Jesus Christ.

Being a great dad begins with understanding how our heavenly Father thinks about us and interacts with us. I can't impart what I don't possess; until I grasp God's leadership, His love, and His role in my life, I will never be able to pass that on to my children.

Years after beginning a relationship with God, I married a wonderful woman who already had two small children. I not only became a new husband, but an instant dad who had no idea what he was doing.

Struggling to learn how to be a father to my children, I decided to write my master's thesis on the role and responsibility of the father in transmitting values to the family. I wasn't very excited about writing a long paper, so I determined to write it in the area where I had the greatest need.

It was fascinating to review the entire Bible concerning the father's role (what he is to be) and responsibility (what he is to do). The result was what I call the biblical portrait of a father and has formed the foundation of my parenting and teaching for the last thirty years.

Here's what a father is to be and do.

1. *He's a leader* (see 1 Corinthians 4:14-16). He makes things happen. He asks questions like, "Where are we now? Where do we need to go? What must we do to get there?"

He focuses on objectives by modeling, taking initiative, setting direction, and making ongoing evaluation. He practices stewardship by being morally responsible for the home before God.

This was new to me; my father didn't lead in our home, and I'd rarely seen this modeled in a positive way. So I wrote down on index cards specific goals for my sons and daughter. I committed to ask God to help me make them holy and conformed to the image of His Son rather than simply happy.

After studying Scripture, I realized I needed to lead my wife in a clear and understanding way if my boys were to see what a godly father looks like. Theresa and I are both first-generation Christians from alcoholic families. It was difficult in the early days to pray out loud together, to spend a few minutes around the supper table sharing a Bible story with our small boys, or to act those stories out after dinner in the living room. My performance orientation and drivenness didn't die easily, but over time we made progress.

As my children got older, the issues changed. Cultural and peer pressure to produce happy children successful in sports, music, and academics were overwhelming at times. We certainly participated in those areas and saw our children grow, but we made some very hard decisions about limiting external activities, rewarding character over accomplishment, and guarding quality time as a family. It required strong leadership. That's what dads do!

2. *He's a priest* (see Deuteronomy 6:1-13). A father makes God known. He asks questions like, "Do my kids know God? Do they have an accurate view of God? Does our home honor God? Are we growing in holiness?"

He focuses on worship—modeling authentic worship, initiating family worship, and encouraging private worship. He's a steward of the home's spiritual climate.

Seeing my role this way was an even more significant challenge than that of leadership. This was completely new territory for me, and I made a lot of mistakes along the way. But as I look back, even my poor attempts made a huge difference in the lives of my children.

When our kids were small I took turns with Theresa tucking them into bed. I would read simple Bible stories and often acted them out. Many times I told stories about my own childhood, which seemed to fascinate my kids and allow them a window into my life and my heart.

I also found that when I made up stories, hearing them was one of my children's greatest delights. Sometimes, not knowing how these tales would end, I'd conclude with a "cliff-hanger" and pick it up the next night. At other times my wife would be mildly perturbed when story time turned into a pillow fight or tickling contest that didn't exactly help the kids get to sleep on time. But my heart bonded with my children, and the fun was followed by praying together about what was on their hearts.

As they got older, we would go out for a Coke or play pickup basketball in the driveway and sit in a pool of sweat talking about what God was teaching them. I would teach my boys the basic verses on overcoming lust, and go to breakfast with my daughter on Sunday as I reviewed my message for the weekend. She'd read her Bible and offer a few tips on how to improve what she'd heard me preach on Saturday night.

What does it mean to be a priest in this sense? It means bringing the reality of Christ to your kids, and taking their needs to the Savior.

3. *He's a teacher* (see Ephesians 6:4). A father imparts wisdom and builds character, asking questions like, "What do my kids need to know, do, and be? How do they learn best? When and how will I teach them in this season of life?"

His focus is on wisdom. He models a biblically centered life and provides formal and informal instruction. He's a steward of the process of transferring godly wisdom to the next generation.

Notice that Ephesians 6:4 says dads are *teachers*; it doesn't say *preachers*. Talking *at* my kids never worked well; but talking *with* my kids and instructing them in creative ways was almost always well received.

In fact, probably the best teaching I ever did with my children happened when they never realized I was instructing them. It was the teachable moment, for instance, when a commercial appeared on the TV screen and I pushed the mute button and asked them what the angle of the commercial was, what it was trying to sell us, why it featured a sexy girl and a rich guy and a cool car. We were learning about the world system and the lust of the flesh, the lust of the eyes, and the pride of life.

At other times the teaching was more formal. I'd like to say we had family devotions every night or morning around the table—but with four kids who were a total of thirteen years apart, that never really worked well for us. We used the dinner table as a more formal teaching time about twice a week; I kept it short, kept it clear, and kept it moving. Most nights I'd ask questions about what they were learning as they read their Bibles, what they encountered in school, or how it was going with friends.

Dinner was a nonnegotiable in our house; we all ate together five or six nights a week. We went to church together as a family, even into our kids' teen years. I believe the common experience was critical. Even though as they got older they might sit with their friends, we often went out to dinner afterward and talked about the message and the service and its application to us as a family.

Before you get to thinking how "spiritual" that is, keep in mind that a good 50 percent of the time my children were cracking jokes and making fun of many of the mistakes I made in my message. They did it in good taste; looking back, I think it was their way of saying, "We know you're just a normal guy, Dad, even though the people at church seem to think you're hot stuff." Normal guys can be teachers, too.

4. *He's a lover* (see Malachi 4:5-6). A father gives people what they need most, asking questions like, "How are my kids really doing? Do they sense my approval and acceptance? Are we connecting at a deep level?"

His focus is on relationships. He models a loving relationship with God and with his spouse; he takes time to provide tender love unconditionally and tough love when necessary. He's a steward of "issues of the heart" at home.

At the end of the day, no dad is perfect. We make lots of mistakes and blow it big-time on occasion. But one of the great truths of fathering is God's promise, "Love covers over a multitude of sins" (1 Peter 4:8).

If there's any single piece of advice I'd offer after raising four very different kids who have all turned out way beyond our expectations, it's this: Love them! Soft love, tough love, but love them.

Be more concerned about what they need than what they want. Be open! Spend time together. Be real! Have fun! Let them know that with you, failure is never final. You get grace, and you can't help but pass it on.

As men, we're called to be intentional about planning for the outcome of our family. We're called to lay down our lives in passionate commitment to the lives He's entrusted to us. No one does it perfectly, but the rewards of partnering with God are huge!

My friendships with my adult kids bring amazing joy to my soul. Few things mean more to me than hearing one of them say, "I love you, Dad."

Watching my children live purposeful lives that shine for Christ assures me they'll spend eternity with Him and our family in heaven. Today *that* is my definition of success.

YOUR CHALLENGE

Help your children understand God's unconditional love by caring for them and carving out time for them. For each child age ten or under, consider committing to spend two or three nights a week putting him or her to bed with a Bible story, hugs, and prayers. Ask your kids what they want to read together or tell one of your own stories. Let them into your life and your heart. As part of this 21-Day Challenge, begin following this pattern tonight or tomorrow night.

If your child is eleven or older, go out for ice cream or miniature golf together and listen to any feelings he or she expresses. Discern what's most important to him or her right now. Take a moment to pray together in the car; then ask good questions and give your undivided attention to the answers.

YOUR PLAN

In the space that follows, come up with a tentative bedtime schedule you think will work with your ten-or-under child. Which days of the week seem best? How long do you want the process to take? What activities would you like to include? Remember, you can always change it later if you need to.

If your child is eleven or older, use the space to list three to five questions you can ask while you're on your outing.

_____

_____

_____

_____

_____

_____

_____

_____

■ ■ ■

CHIP INGRAM is senior pastor of Venture Christian Church in Los Gatos, California. He also serves as president of Living on the Edge, an international teaching and discipleship ministry. The former president of Walk Thru the Bible, he holds an M.S. degree from West Virginia University and a Th.M. degree from Dallas Theological Seminary. His books include *Living on the Edge*, *Overcoming Emotions That Destroy*, and *Effective Parenting in a Defective World*. His teaching reaches more than a million people a week through outlets on the Internet, radio, and television. Chip and his wife, Theresa, have four children and eight grandchildren.

Don't Panic!

BY MICHAEL CATT

Tornadoes. Tsunamis. Cancer. Job loss. Economic uncertainty.

Unfortunately, we aren't immune to the disaster and difficulty that threaten our world globally and our lives personally.

Our kids are fearful today. They're afraid of divorce, disease, disasters, and death. They're surrounded by a 24/7 media cycle, constantly bombarded by bad news. As fathers, it's our responsibility to give them a right perspective in the midst of scary circumstances.

Having been a father for nearly thirty years, I've learned that how I react to the crises and pressures of life directly affects my children. I've had to teach my daughters how to think about tragedy, setbacks, and other events that are beyond our control. As a father, I set the tone in the home. If I panic or give an indication that God can't be trusted, how can I expect my kids to live above fear and live by faith?

Moses' parents had every reason to fear. After an edict was issued by the king of Egypt, demanding that midwives kill all the Hebrew boys they delivered, Moses' parents hid their newborn son. When they could hide him no longer, they placed him in a papyrus basket and set him in the reeds along the bank of the Nile River. They feared the Lord more than the king, and God honored their faithfulness to Him.

Perhaps that's why, when Moses was older and God raised him up to lead the people of Israel out of Egypt, he stood up to Pharaoh and demanded the release of the Israelites. The foundation that Moses' parents stood upon in his infancy was the same foundation Moses stood upon as a grown man.

If our children watch us hide in fear when trouble comes, they too will learn to distrust the Lord. But if they see us stand in the midst of adversity, believing God and holding fast to His Word, they'll be strengthened to stand on their own one day.

I was nearly 40 years old when I learned that I was adopted. Following the initial shock, I struggled for a few years with my identity and the stories I'd been told by my parents. Questions overwhelmed me: *Should I try to locate my birth parents? Why did my parents lie to me all these years? What should I do next?*

My girls were in elementary school at the time. I made sure to work and pray through all of the issues before I shared the news with them. I spent time explaining the situation and reminded them that my parents were still their grandparents, and that would never change. My wife and I maintained a united front during that test, making sure that was reflected to our girls. God gave us the grace to walk that road and to teach our children how to deal with life when faced with an unexpected crisis.

Recently I received a phone call informing me that our home in the mountains had been struck by lightning and had caught fire. We heard various reports that it might be a total loss. My wife and I were grieved and saddened by the news, but her first response was, "The Lord gives, and the Lord takes away. Blessed be the name of the Lord."

In light of this most recent test, my daughter Hayley noted this:

We are adults now, so my parents didn't necessarily have to comfort us. But my dad talked with us about everything he knew after he received the news about the fire. My parents never overreacted. They were focused on the family memories and keepsakes. It wasn't until a few days later that I realized on my own that all of the renovations they had done over the years were ruined. They never mentioned that to me. They spoke of the rocking chair from our nursery, our grandparents' furniture, and other priceless treasures. They never spoke of money or wasted time and effort. They just focused on the memories.

As the father of two grown daughters, I've watched my girls face their own challenges and setbacks with grace and faith. They have honored the Lord, honored their parents, and held fast to the truth of Scripture.

We don't live our lives in isolation. Our response to setbacks will affect not only us, but also those around us. This particularly includes our children. We can't expect them to respond differently or believe God in trials if they watch our faith crumble beneath our worry and panic. Instead, we must help our kids forge a faith that will stand up under pressure by modeling our own fire-tested faith in front of them.

YOUR CHALLENGE

Try one of the following during the next 24 hours:

- If your child isn't too young or unusually sensitive, watch at least ten minutes of a TV news program with him or her, or look through a newspaper or at a news Web site together.

After each story you encounter, ask your child to rate how scary it is on a scale of 1 to 10 (10 being most threatening). Talk about the events that tend to make your child fearful. Are they ongoing dangers like terrorism? Natural disasters like hurricanes? Personal attacks from bullies or burglars? Be ready to share a story about a fear you had as a child. How did you deal with it? What's your perspective now, and how does your faith in God shape your response?

- If your child likes superheroes, spend time together watching an appropriate superhero movie, reading a comic book, or playing with superhero action figures. Ask your child what he or she likes about the hero. If your child were a good friend of the character, would he or she feel safer? Why or why not? Talk about how God is far more powerful than the most invincible superheroes, that He loves us—and, of course, that He's real instead of fictional.

- How can you show your child that panic isn't the best response to crisis? Ask him or her to help you find, through your church or on the Internet, a family or town or country that needs emergency assistance. For example, you might be able to donate to a fund for a child who needs a bone marrow transplant—or a nation in the midst of life-threatening drought. As you lend your aid, talk about how God wants us to meet the unexpected with faith and action, not fear.

YOUR PLAN

After picking one of the aforementioned challenges, outline in the following space how you'll handle the "talking" part of the activity.

What three points would you like to make about your experience with crisis, or how God compares to superheroes, or the better-than-panic actions we can take when trouble hits?

_____

_____

_____

_____

_____

_____

_____

_____

■ ■ ■

MICHAEL CATT is senior pastor of Sherwood Baptist Church in Albany, Georgia. One of the founders of Sherwood Pictures, he has served as executive producer of *Courageous, Fireproof, Facing the Giants*, and *Flywheel*. His books include the bestselling *Fireproof Your Life* as well as *Courageous Living: Dare to Take a Stand* and *The Power of Surrender*. He holds degrees from Mississippi College, Luther Rice Bible College and Seminary, and Trinity Seminary. Michael and his wife, Terri, have two daughters.

Oooh, Tough Word!

BY JIM MOORE

Back in 1998, there was a tragic middle-school shooting in my state of Arkansas. Wanting to head off a similar incident on my children's campus—or any other—I founded an organization called WATCH D.O.G.S. We launched the first program at the school my oldest child attended.

The "D.O.G.S." stands for "Dads of Great Students." Fathers and father figures get involved by volunteering to provide positive role models and strengthen school security. As of July 2011, there are more than 2,100 of our programs in forty U.S. states and New Zealand.

But security isn't all we do—as I proved one day when I was being a "WatchDOG" at my child's school.

My job that day was to mentor children who had little to no working knowledge of the English language. I was given flash cards with words like "cat," "dog," and "ball." There was a word on each card, along with a picture of the item the word referred to.

I would show kids the picture, point to the word, and then pronounce it. Each child would repeat it once after me; then we'd all say it together.

For instance, I'd show my group the word "dog." The rest of the conversation would go like this:

Kid 1: "Dog."

Kid 2: "Dog."

Kid 3: "Dog."

Kid 4: "Dog."

All (unison): "Dog."

This went on for a while, and it went pretty well. But after a string of simple, one-syllable words, some real smart guy at the printer must have thought it would be funny to throw in the word "octagon."

When I saw that word, I inadvertently said out loud, "Oooh, tough word."

Without missing a beat, all four children looking at the picture of an octagon echoed in unison, "Oooh, tough word!"

I couldn't help laughing—on the inside, of course. The purity, innocence, and precious personalities of these children was on display. But then it hit me: This was serious business. My influence was greater than I'd realized. The small sliver of time I had with these kids could be extremely important in their success of grasping the English language.

"WatchDOGS" aren't the only men who have that kind of influence. Every father is in the same spot.

Dad, did you just catch that? We have only a small sliver of time—as measured by the clock of eternity—with our children. That means we have to become extremely focused and serious about guiding our children to be the champions they were created to be!

Talk about challenges! That's a huge one. Fortunately, we have help—including people at organizations like the National Center for Fathering (NCF).

I love NCF. And I love its concept of being a Championship

Father. It's based on sound research which found that a great dad focuses on three fundamentals and tries to live them out in a powerful way.

The three components are *loving*, *coaching*, and *modeling*.

Wow! Think about the impact each of these could have in changing the world if we would simply practice them more consistently in our daily fathering lives!

But let's get something straight—right here, right now. There's no such thing as a perfect dad who does everything without fault—except the heavenly Father that Jesus called "Abba" (Daddy). That's not what Championship Fathering is about. It's about starting to adopt these truths into our families and beginning to accomplish what was described in the very last verse of the very last chapter of the Old Testament: "He will turn the hearts of the fathers to their children, and the hearts of the children to their fathers" (Malachi 4:6).

It starts with us. We're the ones who must turn our hearts to our kids. So why not begin today?

Let's start by making sure we understand the fundamentals.

One of the greatest things God ever gave each of us was an incredible plan for our lives. Jeremiah 29:11 says, "'For I know the plans I have for you,' declares the LORD, 'plans to prosper you and not to harm you, plans to give you hope and a future.'"

Catch those words. God's plans for us are clean, clear, safe, great, and abundant. So should ours be for our children.

What's your plan for your kids? Do you have one yet? If not, begin to construct one today. If you don't have a plan and execute it successfully, the world already has one designed. It's shrewdly and precisely laid out for every kid on the globe. Remember this: Great dads have great plans for their kids.

First of all, a Championship Father is a dad who truly *loves* his family. John 3:16 says, "For God so loved the world that he gave . . ." It's one thing to simply *say* you love your kids, but it's another thing to put that verb, that action word, into practice.

God loves us so much that He gave—and continues to give even to this very second and beyond. Likewise, fathers are called to a love that gives unconditionally and sacrificially, toward their children and their children's mother. We seek to build family members' self-esteem through our presence, encouragement, and regular displays of affection.

Second, Championship Fathers are successful *coaches* to their families.

I love to coach. That was my dream once—to be a college basketball coach. I trained under one of the greatest of all time. I got a chance to be a "walk-on" player—until he watched my talent, or lack thereof, and told me to "walk off"!

Thankfully, he allowed me to stay on as a trainer and student coach my last year. During my four years I learned the game from one of the best teachers. Regardless of what the opposing team threw at us, he always had an answer—because he had a plan, he knew his players, and he taught and trained the right plan into our team until we learned how to execute it and win.

That also describes a successful dad. He is aware of his children's strengths and weaknesses, their interests and their struggles, and he uses those insights every day to help him teach and challenge his kids. He prepares them to win no matter what the opposing team—the world—throws at them.

Much of our coaching comes through the words we speak to our children. Proverbs 18:21 says, "The tongue has the power of life and death, and those who love it will eat its fruit." How are your words, dad? Are they life-giving or life-taking? Are they blessings or are they curses?

Third, a Championship Father is one who *models* the plan and the words he teaches. First John 3:18 says, "Dear children, let us not love with words or tongue but with actions and in truth." John is saying, "Let's don't just talk a good 'love game' to our kids; let's walk it out, too."

How can I attempt to teach my kids one thing but live the opposite? We all know the saying that more is "caught" than "taught." That's not a permission slip giving us the okay to stop teaching. It just reminds us to live out the life, the model we're trying to teach. May our walk match our talk!

Is that challenging enough for you? As those kids in my child's school might say, "Oooh, tough words!"

"Father" can be a tough word, and a tough role to play. But we're not without a map as we face the challenges of being a dad. Concentrating on the three fundamentals can keep us from getting distracted or discouraged—and focused on making the most of that sliver of time we have to influence our children.

 YOUR CHALLENGE

Maybe you're thinking, *Man, I can't live out loving, coaching, and modeling in one day. I'll need a lifetime.*

You're right. So here's the tip I'd like to leave with you. It's a practical way we can all *begin* to accomplish what we're called to do.

Since our modern schedules create a life often lived in "react" mode, let's make a pact that we as dads will rise up in the early morning hours to seek our own Father—our heavenly Father.

We know His plans are good for us. They're to help us prosper. So let's listen to Him as He leads us in the development of His plans for our children.

Let's seek Him early, consistently, and passionately. By setting aside regular time to pray and read His Book—starting during the next 24 hours—let's allow Him to show us how we, as our children's earthly fathers, can mirror Him as we love, coach, and model.

 YOUR PLAN

Perhaps you've already formed the habit of reading the Bible and praying regularly. But if you're like many guys, the idea of regular "devotions" or "quiet times" is about as appealing as quilting. Or you've tried it, like you've tried jogging, and can't seem to keep it up.

For purposes of the 21-Day Challenge, let's make this easy. Sometime before tomorrow night, spend fifteen minutes or so reading 1 Corinthians 13 and asking God to help you apply it to being a dad. It's the "love chapter," after all, and loving is the first fundamental of Championship Fathering.

In the following space, write when and where you'll do this reading and praying. Then use the rest of the space to take notes as you read and pray.

■ ■ ■

JIM MOORE is the founder of WATCH D.O.G.S., the father involvement initiative of the National Center for Fathering. Using humor and life stories, he speaks to groups across the U.S. about reconnecting fathers with their children and about families in general. He has spoken on behalf of the White House and the Department of Education about fatherhood and has appeared on Fox News, *ABC World News Tonight*, and elsewhere. A graduate of the University of Arkansas, Jim has been married for more than twenty-seven years to his wife, Liz. They live in Springdale, Arkansas, and have three children. Jim's mission is to be what he was created to be for the members of his family—"the husband and father they each deserve."

Walking Through Life with Your Kids

BY BRYAN CLAY

Who wouldn't want to be a better dad? How can *I* be a better dad? That's a question I think about a lot.

One way I've found is to create daily opportunities to be physically active with my kids. We have several activities that we enjoy doing together. My favorites are simple: taking a walk or going on a jog.

If you're not a runner or walker, there are many other activities you could choose to do as a family. Hiking, swimming, bike riding, a game of tag, basketball, and even playing catch can be a lot of fun and get everybody off the couch and moving! Kids love these times together and will remember them throughout their lives.

There are three reasons why I feel this is so helpful to becoming a better father.

First, it's a great way to encourage and model a healthy lifestyle for the whole family.

Second, doing these activities with your children creates the perfect opportunity to *talk* with them in a non-stressful, easygoing atmosphere. It's during these fun times that relationships are built.

Third, this is a way for dads to "walk through life" with their children. Be there *for* them and *with* them every day.

When I was a young boy, my parents divorced. I remember the hurt and confusion that came along with that experience. My younger brother and I were forced to navigate some very difficult emotions. Being only ten years old, I didn't know how to deal with or express my feelings, which created many highly volatile situations. I knew one thing: that I was angry!

This anger was not very advantageous in school—or the rest of life. There were times when I faced circumstances that should have left me sad or disappointed, but instead I got angry. Sometimes my anger turned into uncontrollable rage.

It wasn't long before my mom got me into counseling. On the advice of the counselor, Mom gave me the option to run track and field or swim. I chose track and field because wearing a Speedo wouldn't have matched my "tough guy" persona.

Soon after that my mom remarried, which helped our situation as a family but added more confusion to my life. Even after taking the counselor's advice and joining a club track and field team, things continued to spiral out of control.

Trouble seemed to follow me as I joined my high school track team, and then as I entered college. It wasn't until the beginning of my junior year at Azusa Pacific University that God finally grabbed hold of me and shook some sense into me.

Why am I sharing all of this with you? And what's the connection to being physically active with your children?

Here's my answer. I missed out on a lot of fathering because of my parents' divorce. Sure, I had my stepdad, who was a great example of God's unconditional love for me. But as an immature preteen I refused to let my stepdad into my life emotionally. It was just too hard to deal with the divorce. Because of this, God had to father me in other ways and through other people—often involving athletics and other outdoor recreation.

By His grace other men came into my life and helped fill the gap, though there was never a close father-son relationship. There were people like my sixth grade teacher, Mr. Awa, who was the first to flunk me in physical education for failing to turn in written assignments. I still remember a walk we took after class, when he tried to guide me a little by saying, "I know it's tough to understand right now, but you have to know you can't get through life on athletics alone."

There were also people like my junior high school pastor, Rich. When I was fighting with my parents, he occasionally would pick me up from school and take me fishing. Sometimes we wouldn't even talk. We would just stand in chest-high water and let God do the ministering to me.

Then there was my high school coach, Mr. Hee. One day as he was jogging with me around the track, he gave me some advice that later would help me win the 2008 Olympic decathlon gold medal.

"See these gates you pass as you enter the track?" he asked. "When you come in these gates you leave everything in life (frustrations with parents, girlfriend stresses, etc.) outside of them. Nothing you do on the track is going to change any of those situations. When you get done here you'll be able to think clearer and you can go and pick it all back up on your way out."

All of these "fathers" used physical activities to create an unintimidating atmosphere in which to talk and help me. It really is because of these experiences, when men took time to focus on me and walk alongside me through difficult times, that I have become the man I am today.

Maybe you're wondering what the Bible has to say about all this. Surely you remember Hezzalonians 7:75: "When the kids are young, go walking and running with them. Talketh with them between breaths about whatever bothereth them. Giveth to them godly advice and sage counsel that their days might be long and full of good cheer."

Well, maybe not. But there is a pretty important command on this subject in Deuteronomy 11:18-19: "Fix these words of mine in your hearts and minds. . . . Teach them to your children, talking about them when you sit at home and when you walk along the road . . ."

Many dads would agree that they need to "walk alongside" their kids. Today can be your day to start taking that literally.

YOUR CHALLENGE

During the next 24 hours, get involved in a new and regular physical activity with your children. It doesn't have to be a sport, but it certainly can be. Remember to make it enjoyable, not a chore. See it as an experiment, feeling free to change as needed the activity or the time it takes.

Try something that involves plenty of movement and fresh air if possible, but leave the "no pain, no gain" stuff for another time. After all, you want to use this as a chance to talk about your kids' day, their lives, their feelings, their frustrations, their disappointments, and their excitements.

YOUR PLAN

Here are ten ideas for activities you might try. Choose one, or come up with your own. Then, in the space provided, describe when and how often you'll do this—as well as how long you want to try it before evaluating whether a change of course is needed.

1. Walking
2. Jogging
3. Miniature golf
4. Playing catch
5. Running with your dog in a park
6. Gardening
7. Raising chickens
8. Building a treehouse
9. Skateboarding
10. Exercise-oriented video games

_____

_____

_____

_____

_____

_____

_____

■ ■ ■

BRYAN CLAY is a champion decathlete who won the gold medal in the 2008 Beijing Olympics and the silver in the 2004 Athens Olympics. In 2006 he was ranked as the number one decathlete in the world. Bryan has described his faith in Christ as "where I draw my strength." As a speaker and founder of the Bryan Clay Foundation, he encourages character development and motivates kids and adults to make the most of their potential. Bryan attended Azusa Pacific University, where he met his wife, Sarah; they have three children.

Raising Faithful Stewards

BY RANDY ALCORN

Jesus said, "It is more blessed to give than to receive" (Acts 20:35). *The Message* paraphrases it, "You're far happier giving than getting." One of the greatest gifts we fathers can give our children is freedom from materialism.

How? By teaching them to be generous givers who know everything belongs not to them, but to God. And by demonstrating that greater joy is found in giving than keeping.

Giving statistics are bleak. They consistently show that older generations give away a higher percentage of their money than younger ones. We're failing to teach our children to give, and that failure will both rob them of joy and hinder the work of Christ around the globe.

When our girls were seven and five, I gave each of them three jars labeled "Giving," "Saving," and "Spending." Every time they received money from chores or gifts, they were to put at least ten percent into the giving jar, then distribute the rest between the other jars. Once they put money in the giving jar, it was untouchable until they gave it to the Lord at church.

When they put money in "Saving," they could spend it only for something planned. But they were free to transfer money from saving or spending to giving, or from spending to saving.

I'll never forget the night I explained this system to my daughters. They were so excited they immediately distributed the money they already had between the jars. They used those jars for years. This simple system may have resulted in more financial education than anything else my wife Nanci and I did.

Many of us have become so immersed in our culture that we've lost the ability to discern what will—and won't—count for eternity. But Jesus commanded us to store up treasures in heaven, not on earth (Matthew 6:19-21). We put our treasures in heaven by giving to build God's kingdom, not our own.

God entrusts riches to us not to increase our standard of living, but to increase our standard of giving. When Jesus tells us to store up treasures in heaven, He's saying, "You can't take it with you, but you can send it on ahead."

How can we pass these truths to our children? By example.

Two decades ago my family began giving away 100 percent of the royalties from my books. When my youngest daughter was a teenager, we rode our bikes into an expensive neighborhood and admired the biggest, most beautiful house. When I saw the selling price, I said, "If we had kept the royalties from the last year and a half, we could pay cash for that house. Do you wish we would've done that?"

My daughter laughed. "Dad, it's just a house!"

Money didn't have a hold on her. She had learned it all belonged to God, and there was no greater joy than giving it back to Him. Keeping it would have gained us a nice house; giving it gained us an eternal investment.

The more children witness us practicing wise and generous stewardship, the more natural it will seem. If we give generously, save rather than borrow, and spend carefully, we grant our children a wonderful gift—and guard them from financial disaster.

The next generation is growing up amid vast wealth, which many will inherit. Yet most have not learned the habits and joys of giving, saving, and wise spending. If we fathers don't teach our children how to manage God's money, who will?

If you want your children to develop hearts for God, don't overlook what Jesus explicitly says will accomplish that: giving. "Where your treasure is, there your heart will be also" (Matthew 6:21). Our duty is clear: "Bring them up in the training and instruction of the Lord" (Ephesians 6:4).

Some say we shouldn't require our children to give. That makes no more sense than advising, "Don't make your children wash their hands before they eat or wear coats when it's cold."

Others say, "Giving must be from the heart, not imposed."

I respond, "But giving—like Bible study, prayer, and witnessing—is a habit, and all good habits can and should be cultivated." There's no better way for a father to cultivate giving than by making it one of his family's standard practices.

In the movie *Chariots of Fire*, Olympian Eric Liddell says, "When I run, I feel His pleasure." When they give, our children can learn to feel God's pleasure.

Likewise, we can teach our children how to properly manage money by showing them how we spend it. (If you aren't spending it wisely, this could motivate you to change!) By the time children are ten—in some cases younger—they're old enough to learn about the family budget.

Nanci and I occasionally allowed our daughters to spend impulsively. This was difficult. But if we always say no to their unwise decisions, even though children may reluctantly obey, they won't learn wisdom through firsthand experience.

We must be careful not to bail them out or say, "I guess you learned your lesson, so I'll get you what you want." If your child squanders his lunch money, what should you do? Nothing. He must earn more money, use the money he's saved, or go without lunch. If we don't interfere with the natural laws of life, mistakes can be our children's finest teachers.

An alarming number of children growing up in Christian homes are afflicted with the killer disease "affluenza." Consider a typical Christmas in the U.S. After the annual obstacle course through crowded malls, the big day culminates in a pile of abandoned, unappreciated toys. Far from being thankful, children are often grabby, crabby, and ungrateful—because they've been given so much.

Children who grow up getting most of what they want without having to earn it have a predictable future. Odds are they'll misuse credit, blame others, and believe their family, church, country, and employer—if they have one—owe them.

Nothing will interfere more with our children's relationship with God—or prevent them from having one—than a life centered on things. Though many parents seem content to leave their children an inheritance, our job is to leave them a legacy of wisdom and generosity they can pass on to future generations.

An eternal impact can result from our acts of faithful stewardship. That's because we're stewards not just of God's money, but also of the children He entrusts to us.

YOUR CHALLENGE

How can you teach your children the emptiness of materialism in a memorable way? Try taking them to a junkyard or dump. (The lines are short, admission is free, and little boys love it.)

Show them the piles of "treasures" that were formerly expensive presents. Point out things children quarreled about, honesty was sacrificed for, and marriages broke up over. Show them the useless remnants of battered dolls and electronic gadgets.

Explain to them that most of what your family owns will one day end up in a junkyard. Read to them 2 Peter 3:10-14, which tells us that everything in this world will be consumed by fire.

Then ask: "When all that we owned lies broken and useless, what will we have done with our lives that will outlast this world?" Tell your kids you want your life to count for eternity, and that you're praying they'll learn with you the Christ-exalting joy of generous and faithful stewardship.

YOUR PLAN

If you can't get to a dump or junkyard anytime soon, try a thrift store or garage sale—or just lead a safari through your storeroom, closets, or an old toy chest. Point out items that once seemed so desirable but are now abandoned. If that won't work for you in the next 24 hours, use the following space to make a list (with your child's help) of at least five possessions your family used to have but no longer does. Talk about why these items are gone. What did they cost? What was their real worth? How could remembering them help you and your child next time you face a buying decision?

_____

_____

_____

_____

_____

■ ■ ■

RANDY ALCORN is the founder of Eternal Perspective Ministries, a former pastor, and the best-selling author of more than forty books including the novelization of the movie *Courageous, Managing God's Money, Heaven, If God Is Good*, and *Safely Home*. He has spoken around the world, taught on the adjunct faculties of Multnomah University and Western Seminary, and been a guest on hundreds of radio and television programs. Randy and his wife, Nanci, have two daughters and four grandsons.

 For more help in taking today's challenge, scan the symbol with your smartphone. See instructions on page xi in the front of this book. Or visit http://www.21DayDadChallenge.com/Day17.

Improving Their Serve

BY STUART BRISCOE

Many moons ago when our three children were young, we were privileged to be served by an old-fashioned country doctor known affectionately around the area as "Doc Berry." At the time we lived in a small cottage deep in the English countryside, and Doc Berry was a frequent visitor.

He never seemed to pass the house on his rounds (yes, it was in the days when doctors actually visited patients!) without sticking his head around the door and shouting, "Put the kettle on, Jill, I need a cup of tea!" Whatever occupied us when we heard those words was immediately put aside as we greeted our welcome friend and physician.

"I was just driving past," he said one day, "and I was thinking about David's tonsils." David was our eldest child. "Come here, big man," the doctor said to our son, and conducted a brief examination.

Having satisfied himself that nothing of significance was going on in the hidden interior of our boy, Doc Berry turned his attention to his cup of tea. Then he started to dispense practical wisdom.

David's younger brother, a newborn, was at that moment demanding his mother's undivided attention—and receiving it. The doctor surprised us by saying, "Jill, that baby is a guest in this household. But he is allowed to run the show as if he owned it!"

This promptly raised Jill's motherly hackles. Unperturbed, the doctor added, "You and Stuart were together a few years before he appeared on the scene. If all goes well, you will be together for many years after he has moved on. So he is a guest in this house—a deeply loved, welcome guest, but a guest nevertheless. And he must be taught that simple fact right from the beginning. This is for his good as well as yours."

I don't think Jill and I received this piece of advice too readily at the time. It sounded a little cold and callous, and we suspected that taken to its limits it could lead to child neglect. But as the years rolled by, we saw the wisdom of his words.

Jill and I had agreed from the earliest days of our relationship that our motto (for want of a better term) would be based on Joshua 24:15: "As for me and my household, we will serve the LORD." Service was to be the key to our life together, and the whole household would be enrolled in it. But we also knew there is something about being a servant that doesn't always sit well with our innate selfishness. As time went on, we realized that children brought up being tirelessly catered to by adoring parents would grow up thinking the world should do the same for them. The thought of serving the Lord and the world would never occur to them.

So we had a twofold task as parents. We had to love our kids without giving them the impression that they were the only pebbles on the beach, and we had to convey to them that the world owed them nothing—but they were obligated to serve it in the name of the Lord.

We decided the best way to achieve both ends was to take them with us as we served. They would know what we were talking about, catch the vision, and learn the joy of serving.

That's my tip for you today: *Take your kids with you as you serve, and let them learn by serving with you.*

When my itinerant evangelistic work took me away from home and around the world during the early years of my children's up-bringing, I decided that when they graduated from high school their present from me would be a trip around the world. They'd see what I'd been doing and get a feel for the big world they hadn't seen and needed to know and appreciate.

One warm, sultry evening I was preaching in the National The-atre in Singapore. The Singaporeans don't require as much "personal space" as Westerners do, nor do they take up as much square footage. They were packed into the theater by the thousands. At the end of the service, as many sought help with their spiritual lives, David—now eighteen—approached me through the crowd. His face was shining. Normally a man of few words and never effusive, he said, "Dad, this is great! Now I understand! Now I know what you've been doing and why you were gone so much. Dad, it was worth it!"

Two years later I sat cross-legged for hours on a hard floor in a Bangladesh village. I was talking with a small group of village elders who wanted to ask questions about "following Issa" (a reference to Jesus). Since in that culture men and women are kept separate, my daughter, Judy, was seated behind a partition. She listened as these men recounted their lives, detailed their struggles, and outlined their hopes and dreams—and I tried to answer them from the Scriptures.

Sometime later Judy told me she'd been approached by a num-ber of people at her Christian college who offered help if she was struggling with my frequent absence during her formative years.

"Struggle?" she said to them. "I don't struggle with it. I'm proud of him." It was during the night in the Bangladesh village, she told me, that she'd understood that the world did not revolve around her—and that service was to be the theme of her life, too.

Our son Pete has his own stories to tell. Through the grace of God these children—now fifty-two, fifty, and forty-eight years old—know what it is to follow Jesus who said, "The Son of Man did not come to be served, but to serve" (Matthew 20:28). David is an associate pastor, Judy a board member for Compassion International, and Pete a senior pastor—servants all.

YOUR CHALLENGE

Begin teaching your children that selfishness is destructive, service is normative, and sacrifice is not a punishment. Show them what servanthood looks like by doing it with them and modeling it for them.

This is a team effort. If you're married, talk to your wife. Evaluate your lifestyle. Make necessary changes, and start today.

Here's one easy way to begin.

Chances are you can't dive into a full-fledged service project during the next 24 hours. You'd need more preparation time. But you can tackle a smaller challenge like this: Take your child to the supermarket. Give him or her a budget (perhaps $15 to $20) and the assignment of picking out the most food that can be had for that price, which the two of you will take to a food pantry that distributes groceries to the needy. Be sure to choose nonperishable items; you may want to encourage your child to buy things that he or she would appreciate if the situation were reversed.

YOUR PLAN

Brainstorm some longer-term service opportunities with your child. Are there any elderly or disabled people in your neighborhood who need help with chores? Is your church planning a local outreach event or mission trip? Is there a nursing home nearby that gets few visitors? How about joining in a fast or hike or car wash to raise money for earthquake victims or fund your church's youth program? Write your ideas in the following space; then prioritize them in order of their importance to the two of you.

_____

_____

_____

_____

■ ■ ■

STUART BRISCOE is a popular Bible teacher, author, and founder of the Telling the Truth ministry. Born in 1930 in England, he has been preaching since he was seventeen. In 1959 he married Jill, who would also become a sought-after writer and speaker. In 1970 he became a pastor at Elmbrook Church in Wisconsin, where he served for thirty years. He and Jill continue to serve as Elmbrook's ministers-at-large, traveling the globe to help churches and missionaries. Stuart has written more than forty books, preached in more than one hundred countries, and received honorary doctorates from a number of schools and universities. He and Jill have three children and thirteen grandchildren.

Helping Kids Learn Responsibility

BY LEE PARIS

Oh, those precious years between the terrible twos and the terrible teens! The days when the sound of father opening the front door ignites adoring children to open their arms and fly into the returning dad, smothering him with hugs, kisses, and offers to obey his every command.

Well, perhaps such father fantasies are not an everyday fulfillment. But for me, it was more often than not.

By simply opening the door to our home, I was the long-awaited hero to my kids. The hours before bed were spent rolling on the floor in tickling glee, dearly remembered dinners deliciously prepared by mom, baths with more laughs than suds, bedtime stories, and prayers. I adored my children and they me.

Such would "surely follow me all the days of my life."

Surely not.

One day the music playing on the headset drowned out the sound of the door I came through. One day they were at a friend's house and not there to greet me.

Ball practice and study groups replaced our utopian family rituals. My once never-questioned authority was oft second-guessed, disputed, or simply disobeyed. My precious children had become teenagers, adolescents, challenges!

When facing a challenge of any nature we must have effective tools. I had in my toolbox the usual: the hammer of fatherly authority, the nails of punishment, the pliers of coercion. But these just didn't seem to produce many constructive results with my teenage kids.

Committed to them and to my responsibility, I sought God's guidance through the shield of faith and the sword of the Spirit and prayers through the night. He caused me to look under the usual tools, digging deeper into the box for some that could and would bless my children and help me meet the challenge of being a father to teenagers in twenty-first-century America.

I hope some of these tools may be helpful to you in your journey, whether you have teens at the moment or not.

Whether a great blessing or an added challenge, our family lived in a neighborhood, worshiped at a church, and attended a school where affluence was—while not universal—prevalent. The norm was to buy the latest, from fashion to vehicles, for our children with little or no requirements from them. I refer to this as "welfare parenting."

Don't get me wrong. I believe we should sacrificially serve and provide for our children. We also have a responsibility to care for others who are unable to care for themselves. Yet discernment is needed so that we don't destroy incentives for those who are able to work and provide. A dad should pray as Solomon did: "So give your servant a discerning heart to govern your people and to distinguish between right and wrong" (1 Kings 3:9).

As in homes around us, talk began at ours: "What kind of new car are you going to get me, Dad?"

Not wanting to bow to significant pressure around me, I found in the bottom recesses of my toolbox a method designed to help our oldest child earn a relatively new car in a nontraditional way. I wrote her a letter expressing my awareness of her deep desire for a vehicle, of my desire to help her "finish strong" before leaving the nest, and of a way to provide a "molding method to be continued long after the car is earned."

She would be paid in Monopoly money for her efforts in many areas including appearance, attitude, and her help with our family and others. This included weekly payment for errands run for her mom, meal preparations and cleanup, time helping her younger sister, and other special extensions of help at home.

At school she could earn Monopoly money not only for successful grades but also for acts of mercy, discipleship, notes of encouragement, and more. Writing letters to those in need or on the mission field was rewarded, too. To encourage her spiritual growth, benefits were offered for time in God's Word, consistent prayer documented in her journal, and time spent receiving godly counsel. A reward also was extended for establishing her life plan.

Each week she would submit to me an invoice with evidence of her accomplishments. She could continue as long as she wanted until high school graduation, saving up for a better car. Before long I had to buy a new Monopoly set to get more "cash," which she would eventually trade for the real thing.

Just as I am not a dad without flaws, the method was not without its shortcomings. It did, however, serve her well.

Regrettably, the plan had limited success with our son. At age sixteen he cashed in at $2,000, earned $2,000 in a job, and bought a very used hand-me-down from a close friend.

Then came college. I should explain that my son is incredibly gifted. He is exceptionally handsome, smart, and likeable. In college he decided to major in *fun*. I love fun. I love watching him have fun. The major, however, concerned me.

After seeking the Lord and His creativity, I told my son I could not decide for him his commitment to education. I further explained, though, that I could direct the use of funds I provided him, and that a college education was a privilege and not something I owed him.

We eventually consummated a college contract whereby his first semester was totally paid for, including necessities and "recreational" allowances. From then on he could decide how we were to be involved in his education. At a minimal passing level—a C average—we would provide his tuition funds. At slightly above C level, additional fraternity and date money would be added. With a B average, more could be earned toward a new car and other desires. This was designed not only as a deterrent to failure but also as a reward for success. Sounded like the real world to me.

For most of college, the plan worked. There was one semester that required really tough love. There were even days without food that broke his mother's heart.

Today my son is in his twenties, has a great job in the real world, and is making monthly payments on his own shiny, almost-new car. He understands the meaning of work and is equipped to do it. He may have learned these without our college plan, but the plan helped me fulfill my obligation to him as a father.

I realize that paying for cars and colleges is not within the reach of every parent. But this plan could work for lower-priced goals, too—a school trip or cell phone, for example. It could work for pre-teens, too; your child may not be old enough for a car, but may desire a new bike or video game. Monopoly money or a substitute could be earned toward these as well.

The goal is to teach our children the cost of material things they want and the value of working toward the goal of acquiring them. Working together binds dad and child through interaction, cooperation, and the shared joy of accomplishment.

I honestly believe my children, having worked through our plan, have a deeper appreciation for the hours I work to provide for our family. The plan certainly gave me much more satisfaction in helping them financially, knowing they had contributed while learning powerful life lessons.

I think our heavenly Father desires to give us many things that are shiny and new. Yet He is much more interested in molding our hearts and equipping us for His service and for eternity. I shudder to think of the price He paid for our greatest gift. We as parents should look to Him as we seek to love and guide our children, and be willing to pay the price this love requires.

Later in our parenting journey the Lord blessed us with our third child. Whether due to wisdom gained from our experience, her unique genetic makeup, or just God's mercy toward us aging parents, our youngest came up with her own plan. As creative as my wife and I had to be with our first two, with the third it was a less difficult process.

All children are uniquely and wonderfully made—and require great love and effort. We have a heavenly Father who forgives us when we err and is ready to give us the tools we need with each new day. May He bless you as you use those tools to take on the challenge of guiding your child toward responsibility.

YOUR CHALLENGE

Pray, as King Solomon did, for the Lord to give you discernment. Ask Him what outside-the-box incentive plan might be helpful in this challenge called fathering.

Schedule a meeting with your child during the next 24 hours. Tell him or her that you have a business deal to propose.

Find out what kind of goal your child would like to save up for this week—perhaps limiting it to a $25 purchase. Together, create an earning opportunity that will cover that amount.

For a longer-term goal, work together to design a plan for a larger shared dream. Create a strategy that helps motivate, mold, and equip your child for the next chapter of his or her life. Follow the plan—and stay on your knees!

YOUR PLAN

Use the following space to take notes on your meeting with your child. You'll want to include details of the plan—how money is earned and at what rate, whether the goal can be changed in midstream, what happens if the goal isn't reached in time, etc.

_____

_____

_____

_____

_____

_____

_____

■ ■ ■

LEE PARIS is chairman of the National Center for Fathering. He is also an attorney and chief executive officer of Meadowbrook Capital, L.L.C. in Jackson, Mississippi. A graduate of the University of Mississippi and the University of Mississippi School of Law, he founded Mission Mississippi, an organization that encourages and expresses unity across racial and denominational lines. He is chairman of the Mississippi Charitable Foundation, a former director of Patrick Morley Ministries, chairman of the Young Presidents' Organization's Christian Fellowship Network, and a deacon in his church. He and his wife, Lisa, have three children.

Be a Storyteller

BY MARCELLUS CASEY

One of my favorite things to do with my father when I was growing up was to listen to him tell me stories. I would be consumed with playing a video game or watching television when Dad would ask me, "Hey, Son, would you like to take a ride in the car with me?"

We would head out in the car aimlessly. But the more we took these drives, the more I grew accustomed to a pattern. We'd roll down the windows, turn up the music, grab a snack from the gas station, and drive for a long time. Chili hot dogs and a soda were my favorite refreshment as old-school funk music thumped through the car and threw my dad into his rhythm of storytelling.

We had great drives around our neighborhood in Chicago, but the best were around my grandparents' house in Virginia. That was because I could buy a soda in a glass bottle there. I didn't have the luxury at home of popping off the bottle cap at the gas station counter like I could in Salem, Virginia.

Dad's stories seemed to come alive when we were in Salem. As soon as we started driving down the hill past the old cemetery, he began telling me about his glory days as a high school football player.

By the time we grabbed our snack at the gas station at the bottom of the hill, he was already telling me how he scored five touchdowns in one game.

Then we'd hop in the car and look back at that steep hill and he would pause. He'd reminisce about how he and my uncle ran sprints up the hill to get in shape for football. He told me everything. We'd drive past the football and baseball fields, stopping to play catch. When I got older we'd even use these fields to train for my upcoming high school and college football seasons.

As the day went on, we'd roll past the old Baptist church as we headed downtown. After a few turns we'd go through some of the nicest neighborhoods. We'd slow down in front of some of the houses where his high school teammates had lived.

The car would creep past these houses. Oddly, though, the stories that came out were more about my grandmother than about Dad's teammates. He explained that his mother had cleaned these houses during the day to make ends meet. It was hard for me to imagine my gray-haired, distinguished grandmother on her hands and knees scrubbing someone else's house. Could it be the same woman I'd seen singing in her beautiful choir robes in front of a packed church? Those stories of her hard work and perseverance taught me there will never be a job that is beneath me if it's going to provide for my family or help other people.

We'd drive past the Veterans Administration hospital where my grandfather had worked. In the parking lot Dad would point out the baseball field at the bottom of the hill. He'd tell me how my grandfather took breaks between shifts to watch my father play ball. Dad seemed to be telling me that taking an interest in your children is something a man should always do.

I hadn't known my grandfather really well. But my father told me so many stories about him that he quickly became a giant hero in my heart. I heard all the accounts of his hard work, his faithfulness as a deacon in the church, and his care for my father. It gave me guidelines and expectations of where my priorities needed to be when I stepped into manhood.

My father's stories weren't confined to his own hometown. On family vacations we would also visit High Point, North Carolina, where my mother had grown up. My dad and I would drive past the building where Mom's dad had started his own dental practice. Dad would tell me how my grandfather was the first African-American man to own his own dental practice in High Point—as well as a leader for the African-American community who helped to integrate the school system.

Then we'd drive past the house where my mother grew up. My father would tell me about the time he sat down with Grandfather to ask him for my mother's hand in marriage. I'd listen intently as my father explained how nervous he was in that conversation because of the way he looked up to my grandfather. I'd wonder if I could ever have the courage to ask a man for his daughter's hand.

My father's stories have guided me through life. They provided a real backdrop for the scriptural lessons he taught me later. When I grew older and started to read the Bible, I began to understand the importance of the hundreds of stories my father had told me over and over again.

Stories are about remembering. In the book of Joshua, God told people to remember His faithfulness. His special people had spent hundreds of years in slavery and decades wandering in the desert trying to find their home. Now God was miraculously guiding them into the land He'd promised them. He wanted them to remember the amazing things He was doing. After He miraculously split open the Jordan River and His people crossed over on dry land, He commanded the leaders to do something unique. He told them to take stones from the bottom of that dry river so that they could build an altar of remembrance.

Joshua 4:21-23 says, "In the future when your descendants ask their fathers, 'What do these stones mean?' tell them, 'Israel crossed the Jordan on dry ground.' For the LORD your God dried up the Jordan before you until you had crossed over." God wanted His people to build their future on recalling His faithfulness in the past. My father would drive me around for hours telling me miraculous stories of God's faithfulness. What I now realize is that he was handing me stones of remembrance upon which I could build my future.

Become a storyteller. For the sake of your children's future, communicate to them the faithfulness of God in your past.

YOUR CHALLENGE

Your kids have questions: "Who is my dad? What is in his past? Is my dad a real person? Will I be like my dad?"

Don't be afraid to tell your stories to your kids. I didn't always understand why my dad told me so many stories, but it helped me to understand his and our family's past. My father would even tell me about the times when he messed up, when he'd blown it.

I encourage you to carve out fifteen or twenty minutes today to open up to your kids and let them understand you. Give them something to remember, a way to see what God has done in your life. It will guide them and put flesh onto biblical advice that otherwise might be hard for them to connect with.

YOUR PLAN

What's a good place for you to be alone with your kids to tell them parts of your story? What are some lessons you've learned that your kids will benefit from knowing?

How well do your kids know *your* parents? Are there funny stories or photo albums you can explore that will help your kids see that you're a real person?

Don't rush. Just pick a few stories that will connect your kids to the things they need to hear. Give the stories titles and write the titles in the following space.

_____

_____

_____

_____

_____

_____

_____

_____

_____

■ ■ ■

MARCELLUS CASEY is the Champaign-Urbana area director of the Fellowship of Christian Athletes (FCA) as well as the chaplain for the University of Illinois men's football team and coordinator for all sport chaplains on the campus. He is passionate about reaching out to athletes and coaches with the gospel of Jesus Christ. The son of Carey Casey, Marcellus attended Northwest Missouri State University, where he played football for two years and led FCA Chapel for two years. Marcellus and his wife, Stephanie, have two daughters.

For more help in taking today's challenge, scan the symbol with your smartphone. See instructions on page xi in the front of this book. Or visit http://www.21DayDadChallenge.com/Day20.

Holding Kids Accountable

BY CAREY CASEY

When I was about thirteen, my buddies and I used to play cards together. They weren't heated games with high stakes or anything; we were just having fun. But there were other things going on that could have had major implications for our future and our character.

See, sometimes one of my friends would bring his deck of cards with pornographic images on them. We thought we were cool playing our card games with those. Then, when the game was over, each of us grabbed four or five of the cards to take home with us.

Now, I hope you aren't too shocked about this. I was a churchgoing kid and did fine in many ways, but in this area I let my guard down during those moments. I was shortsighted; my desire to be cool and one of the guys became more important than my long-term character, and I got off track. I imagine something like that happened at some point in your early years.

I took those cards home and hid them inside the pages of a sports magazine that I kept in the headboard of my bed—very well hidden, I thought. But wouldn't you know it? My pop found them.

I'll never forget the look on his face and what he said when he came to me with those cards. I was so embarrassed and ashamed—and a bit put out that he'd gone through my stuff, as I'm sure many kids would be. Dad was disappointed, but he didn't lose his mind. He held those cards out and said, "Son, we don't look at these things. *This is not who we are.*"

Something similar happened when I was a senior in high school. I had some success on the football field and received attention from some university football programs. (If you've heard shady things about college sports recruiting today, I'd say it was even worse back then.) I really wanted to play big-time football and knew that some major universities were looking at me. But I hadn't worked hard enough in class and didn't qualify academically.

During our banquet at the end of the year, an assistant coach from one university came over to talk to me. I knew I faced some pretty big hurdles, but this coach said, "Carey, don't worry about it. We got it all under control; we've got you qualified for school."

I was willing to play along. "Sounds great!" I said.

I thought my dad was off somewhere else, but he was right behind me. Quickly he said, "No, he *didn't* qualify." Then he added, "No, Carey's going to prep school or junior college."

I was thinking, *Quiet, Dad! No! I can go and play Division I my freshman year; I can be playing on TV!*

But my dad saw through all that, and reeled me in.

I ended up going to junior college in a small town, and I had a great experience. I did well on the football field, but mostly I grew up as a person. I developed good study habits and disciplines I'd never picked up in high school—and probably wouldn't have developed at a big university. And I became a leader on campus.

If my daddy hadn't stood up for what was right, I could easily have gone straight to a four-year college without qualifying. I could have cheated and played football. But now, knowing who I was back then, chances are I would have flunked out and squandered the greater opportunities of a college education. I can see how my dad protected me from those dangers, and really protected me from myself.

Has anything like that happened to you? I sure hope so. I hope you had a dad or a father figure who held you accountable, checked up on you, and set you straight.

Too many kids today don't have that fatherly influence in their lives. They aren't confronted about bad behavior or coached about good behavior, and they grow up thinking things that are wrong really aren't that bad. Their friends or their own curiosity lead them further and further off course.

Proverbs 19:18 says, "Discipline your son, for in that there is hope; do not be a willing party to his death." That discipline will include some correction and punishment to help teach kids important lessons, and different methods will work better at different stages.

There's no substitute for holding our children accountable for their actions. As fathers, we need to be that backup conscience to keep them on the right path until their own consciences become more reliable.

Today I see those two events in my life as important turning points—times when I could have kept going down a path that would have led me to a life of selfishness, disobedience, and ultimately destruction. But thanks in large part to that coaching from my pop, I turned back and took a narrower road that brought me to a better life that God had in store for me.

I can hardly imagine how my life would be different today if I'd have gone through it thinking that looking at pornography was no big deal—or that bending the rules is okay if it helps you get what you want.

My pop was no SuperDad. He didn't take us on extravagant

vacations or pay for us to travel the world, and he didn't teach me a foreign language or a musical instrument. He wasn't a pastor or an expert in child psychology. He never went to college. He wasn't famous. He worked a blue-collar job for pretty much his whole life.

He was as common as the day is long. But if there's one word I'd use to describe him, it's *faithful*—to his family, to God, and to God's purpose for his life.

What he did for me wasn't miraculous. He simply was involved enough and aware enough of what I was doing—and where I was vulnerable—that he noticed when I strayed from the path or took a wrong turn. He had the courage to speak up and confront sins. In so doing, he created huge, memorable lessons that helped to shape my character.

Dad, I hope you'll have the courage to stand up for what's right and say, "No. This is not who we are." Or, "If you go down that road, the outcome will not be good." Your kids might get mad at you for the moment, but their future and their character are worth it—especially when they could be heading toward something dangerous.

There's one more hope I have for you. If you're into an activity that could threaten your character or your family—pornography, for instance—consider this a friendly confrontation from a father figure in your life: *That isn't who you are.* God has something better for you if you'll trust Him in that area.

YOUR CHALLENGE

If you're going to tell your child, "This is not who we are"—or something similar that calls him or her to a higher standard—you need to clearly define that standard. The most important way to do that is to model it; demonstrate those virtues and values every day.

But it also helps to spell it out for your children. Do you have a family mission statement? Have you written and discussed the principles and values your family stands for?

It's a great exercise, and you can start it during the next 24 hours. Have each family member contribute ideas, and include appropriate Bible verses. Write it down (a paragraph to a page should be plenty) and post it prominently. Then come back and review it—and revise it if necessary—at least once a year.

 YOUR PLAN

Once you've completed your family mission statement, here's a longer-term project.

In order to hold your children accountable, you need to know how they're doing—how they function, their hopes and dreams, their strengths and weaknesses. Answer these questions about each of your kids using the following space—and feel free to get help from your children's mother. Insights like these will strengthen many areas of your fathering.

- What were your child's greatest achievements and disappointments in the past year?
- In what areas is he strong?
- Where is he vulnerable?
- What key challenges or temptations is she likely to face in the next six months?

- What positive and negative habits is she picking up from her friends?
- Who are your child's heroes, and what are some likely outcomes of emulating those people?

_____

_____

_____

_____

_____

_____

_____

_____

■ ■ ■

CAREY CASEY is CEO of the National Center for Fathering, head-quartered in Kansas City, and the author (with Neil Wilson) of *Championship Fathering: How to Win at Being a Dad*. Speaking across the U.S. and around the world, Carey encourages and equips men to be the fathers their children need. He has served as a chaplain for NFL football teams and the U.S. Olympic team, and as an inner-city pastor in Chicago. For eighteen years Carey was on staff with the Fellowship of Christian Athletes, serving as national urban director and president of the FCA Foundation. Carey and his wife, Melanie, have four children and five grandchildren.

Afterword

BY CAREY CASEY

Each of the chapters in this 21-Day Challenge has focused on how to help you be the father and husband God has called you to be. I'm sure you agree that this is important stuff.

When you're a father who's there for his children, your whole family changes. You give your kids a great chance to succeed. You're there to tell a son, "This is how you carry yourself," and, "This is how you do chores with excellence," and, "Son, I love you, but we don't do that, and here's why." You're there to make sure your daughter understands how she's supposed to be respected and cherished.

If someday you can look back on your life and see close relationships with family members who are serving Christ and showing His love to others, that's a fantastic legacy. It's a great goal to keep in mind during your day-to-day fathering challenges.

But no matter how great a dad you are and no matter how well your children may be doing, there's a bigger picture of fatherhood you can't ignore. Outside the walls of your home, many children *aren't* getting what they need from their dads.

Satan knows how important a father's role is. Taking down dads is part of his strategy, and he's had some success in our society and our world. Maybe that's part of the penalty described in Malachi 4:6: "He will turn the hearts of the fathers to their children, and the hearts of the children to their fathers; or else I will come and strike the land with a curse."

I'll never forget the night my oldest daughter had her first baby. It was memorable for many reasons. My bride Melanie and I actually arrived at the hospital before my daughter and her husband. Due to remodeling in the building, maternity patients had to go through the emergency room, so that's where we were. In the waiting room were about twenty young men—mostly African American, dressed as you'd expect to see urban teenagers dressed.

When my daughter and her husband pulled up, I offered to park their car while the hospital staff whisked them away. Coming back inside, I suddenly was surrounded by a huge commotion—disarray like you would not believe. Those young men were running around, cursing in anger, punching holes in walls and breaking windows, creating total chaos. I was right there in the middle of it, though they didn't seem to notice me.

Before long I discovered that they were there for a young man who'd been shot. They had just learned that he'd died.

As I watched, it struck me: There was no older male—a father or father figure—to help them through this. The young man's mother was there, but there was no positive influence or wise counsel from a mature male.

I asked the staff if there was any way I could help. But to them I could have been anybody, and they declined.

Eventually I rejoined my family members, but that scene stayed in my mind. Where were the adult males who could bring sense to all that was going on? I also couldn't help but notice the contrast between those angry young men and my own grandson who was being born to his mother *and his father*. Because of that, my grandson has a great chance to win in life.

For me, that was a powerful, real-life picture of the crisis we're facing.

The statistics can't be ignored. Did you know that in the U.S. alone, more than twenty million children live in father-absent households? That's more than one out of four, and there are tragic consequences: Fatherless children are about five times more likely to live in poverty and two to three times more likely to have emotional and behavioral problems. They're twice as likely to drop out of school, three times more likely to commit suicide, and more likely to suffer physical and mental disorders, commit criminal acts, engage in premarital sex and get pregnant, and use drugs and alcohol.

It isn't a pretty picture, and I'm sure you see examples on your street of the millions of children struggling with issues connected to father absence. *Fatherlessness is a crisis.* I say those words and cite those statistics all the time as I travel and speak, almost to the point that it feels the message is getting old. But I have to keep doing it; sad as it is, people need to know what's happening.

The numbers always blow people away. Many haven't realized what we're up against.

Please don't skim past those statistics without really thinking about them. *More than twenty million children* are facing tough odds in many areas of life, and that's only in the U.S. Not all of them will struggle; many will overcome their situation and do fine. Still, we're talking about millions of children.

If a disease or natural disaster threatened even ten million kids, there would be worldwide panic and outrage. Public figures would be urging everyone to take action. Leaders would rally us to "save the children, our most precious resource." It would be that kind of emergency.

Yet the fatherhood crisis doesn't seem to spark that kind of concern. Maybe people have learned to expect less of fathers and just accept the fact that so many aren't there. But *it is a big deal*. As Psalm 68:5 states, God cares deeply for the fatherless; He is a "father to the fatherless, a defender of widows."

Are there kids you know who don't have the benefit of a dad to guide them through the storms of life? If you're a man of character and want to make a difference, reach out to a child in need.

Recently I've heard three amazing stories about men who are doing this, and they inspire me. These men are heroes.

Tony is thirty-one, with two young children. Some time ago, a new family came to his church—a mom and several children. Most people at that church are Caucasian, but this family was African American. The mom and her kids attended for a few weeks, then stopped.

Tony wondered why. He contacted the mom and connected with one of her sons, a sophomore in high school. The boy had lost his dad at age thirteen, and Tony could tell he really needed some attention and a man's direction. With the mother's blessing, Tony began taking the boy with him on Saturdays to work on a farm outside the city—and paying him a good wage. The two of them also talked just about every day after school.

Tony helped the boy open a bank account and coached him about money management. This high school kid now has over $600 put away. More than that, he's learning about saving and self-discipline—things that many high schoolers surely need to learn these days.

When the boy had trouble getting to school on time, Tony took him to buy an alarm clock and talked about how to get organized in the morning. That's the stuff a father does, and Tony—a white man with two really young kids—stepped in to do this for a black teenager who needed a dad.

Another story comes from Greg, a good friend of ours at the National Center for Fathering. For some time he's been committed to helping us inspire and equip dads, but recently his eyes were opened even more to the power and potential of a father figure.

Greg is on a leadership committee for his children's Christian school. During one recent meeting the discussion revolved around Brett, a seven-year-old boy who'd recently been suspended from the school for behavior issues.

Greg didn't know Brett, but his children did. He heard the tragic story of Brett's father, who'd died suddenly of a heart attack only months before. Brett's dad had been very loving and dedicated to his family and to Christ, and the boy's difficulties hadn't started until he lost his father. During the meeting, Greg expressed his concern for the boy. Surely there was something they could try to help the child, he thought.

The committee decided to pray about it, and the principal prayed specifically for someone to step up as a father figure for Brett. During that prayer Greg felt a clear, powerful call from God that *he* was the one to step into the gap. So Greg contacted Brett's mother and asked if he and his twelve-year-old son, Jack, could take Brett for a "boys' day out." The mother was overwhelmed and wept.

With his family's full support, Greg and his son came up with a list of twenty things a seven-year-old would like to do. On a Sunday afternoon they picked up Brett and took him to play basketball and swim. They shot off rockets and chased trains. More than once Greg heard Brett say, "These are things me and my dad used to do."

At the end of the day, Greg gave Brett his cell phone number and let the boy know he would always be there for him. "Call me anytime," Greg added.

Since that day, Brett has called just about every day. He waits to see Greg when Greg drops off his own kids for school. Greg often tells the boy, "I'm not your dad, but your dad would be proud of you and the good choices you continue to make."

The best part is that Brett's performance and behavior issues at school have turned around. The anger and despair have been replaced with a growing level of joy for all concerned. Greg says, "My family will never be the same since we engaged in the life of this young boy."

I recently heard from another dad, Doug, who accompanied his son on a kindergarten field trip. Doug was the only male chaperone, and it quickly became clear that many of the kids craved his attention. They gravitated to him, asking questions and hanging around to see what he would do or say.

For that day, those kids had a father figure. Doug saw it firsthand, and now he's even more convinced that involved and caring dads can make a difference in the lives of children who need them.

That's the power of a father figure. Men who see a need and fill the gap are an important part of changing the culture by encouraging other kids. I hope you see that there are kids around you who need that fatherly presence in their lives, and I hope you'll step up, too.

I believe that in the near future similar opportunities will come your way—especially now that you're more aware of the issue. Wherever you are—at your child's school, church, a youth sports event, or somewhere else—kids who need a dad will gravitate toward you.

So don't be surprised! Expect these kinds of things to happen, and be ready. You have father power whether you realize it or not, and a lot of kids are hungry for it. They may be black, white, brown, urban, suburban, or whatever. You may be in situations where you can give hope and encouragement to a young person who desperately needs it.

Like Tony, Greg, and Doug, you can step up and do something for other Bretts out there. As these men demonstrate, it isn't rocket science. Anyone, including you, can reach out to fatherless kids.

Will it take some of your time? Yes, but probably not as much as you think. It just requires a little awareness, making yourself available, and showing you care. You can speak a word of encouragement and provide a listening ear or an arm around the shoulder.

If you really want to make a difference, be a father figure. I know there's a kid near you who needs a real man in his or her life. If we fathers all do this, we have the power to literally change our culture. We can set up not only our own children, but future generations of children, for much greater success.

BONUS CHALLENGES

The road to better fathering doesn't stop here! Keep your momentum going with the following challenges from Dr. Wayne Gordon and Dr. Ken Canfield. As Joe White says, "It's never too late to start. It's always too early to quit."

Listening Up

BY DR. WAYNE "COACH" GORDON

When our kids were growing up in the 1980s, we had a rule in our house about gym shoes: Mom and Dad would pay only $40 for them. If the kids wanted to buy something more expensive, they had to contribute their own money. Even with their contribution, we still wouldn't purchase any footwear over $60.

We didn't come to this position without the kids' input. We did it by listening to them and trying to empathize with them in their situations. One day our daughter had come home wearing her fairly new, clean gym shoes. All her friends, who wore L.A. Gear shoes, had made fun of her because she was wearing a no-name brand. Anne and I listened to her and talked through her feelings of embarrassment and hurt.

In the case of our son Andrew, the process took a little longer. A status symbol for him was Air Jordans, with a price tag of $100. They couldn't just be any Air Jordans, either; they had to be that year's *style* of Air Jordans.

One day Andrew and I went to the mall to shop for shoes. He saw the pair he wanted and I saw the price tag. "No way," I said.

"You know the rules, and we will not spend $100 on shoes. But we can shop around and see if any stores sell Air Jordans at a lower price."

We walked through the entire mall without success. "You're going to have to get a different kind of shoe," I finally said.

He resisted. I tried to stay calm, but then I got angry. I pointed to a pair of less-expensive shoes and said, "Are you going to get these shoes or not?"

"No!" he snapped, and we charged out of the mall. We rode home in silence.

Later that night I went into his bedroom to pray with him, as was our custom. "Andrew, what is the thing with these gym shoes?" I asked. "Do gym shoes make you a better person?"

"No," he answered. "But when you have those shoes on, everybody looks at you, and they know you're in style. It makes me feel good." He started to cry. "If I don't wear those shoes, everyone will make fun of me!"

"Maybe they will," I replied. "But the important thing is what is inside of you: your love for people and your love for God. If you grow up looking to wear the best suit, drive the best car, and live in the best house, you'll be miserable."

Hoping my little sermon had won him over, I asked, "What do you think?"

"I still want the Air Jordans."

"Well, you can't have them," I concluded. "If you want to get the other shoes, let me know." And I walked out of the room.

Early the next morning, I went to my office at the church to have devotions. The phone rang, and it was Andrew. "Dad, I thought some more about it last night and you're right. I want to get the $60 gym shoes instead."

That battle ended on a positive note, though they don't all end so well. If I hadn't listened to Andrew, I'm not sure he and I would have been able to come to some agreement. Listening helped him to feel valued and to be assured that we love and care for him.

Listening is one of the things that's kept our family close. I've had the tremendous blessing of being married to my wife, Anne, for thirty-four years as I write this. Together we've raised our three children—Angela, Andrew, and Austin—in the inner city of Chicago. We've chosen to live here because of our calling to ministry in North Lawndale where I pastor Lawndale Community Church.

Often people have thought this to be unwise because of the danger and disadvantages of our community. Actually, Anne and I have found the opposite to be true. Growing up here has helped our children to become wonderful Christian adults; all three live and work in the city. Being here has helped us to be close as a family.

So has listening to each other. It's been one of the most important values in our household. We've tried to listen to our children and to value their thoughts and opinions on all things.

That can be painful, though. And hazardous to my status quo.

Several years ago while we were on vacation, Anne and I asked our two oldest children, who were eight and ten at the time, "If there was one thing you could change about us, what would it be?"

"Well, Mom, sometimes you get a little irritable," one of the kids said. "It would be nice if you wouldn't yell at us when you get mad."

I breathed a sigh of relief, and not just because I hadn't been mentioned yet. *It sounds like we're doing okay. Every parent flies off the handle every once in a while.*

Then it was my turn. My son said, "Dad, I want you to be home more at night. You're never around. I never get to see you."

That hurt, but it wasn't a surprise. "Andrew, that's certainly a good point," I said.

Next it was Angela's turn: "Dad, I wish you were someone I could trust. I don't trust you."

I was stunned. "What do you mean?" I asked.

"You tell me you're going to do something, but you don't do it. You break your promises."

She was right. I had the best of intentions toward my children, saying things like, "I'll read you a book tonight, Angela," or "We'll go to the lake tomorrow," or "I'll be home in time to help you with your homework." But then I would let church business and people in need take priority over my family members and their needs.

I learned so much from Angela and Andrew in that instant. I clearly had been putting the ministry of the church ahead of my family. That night changed my life; I've attempted to lead my life much differently since then. It's still hard for me to put my family ahead of ministry, but the lessons I've learned by listening to my children have had a deep impact on my priorities.

Kids can teach us some pretty important things, as Jesus pointed out: "At that time the disciples came to Jesus and asked, 'Who is the greatest in the kingdom of heaven?' He called a little child and had him stand among them. And he said: 'I tell you the truth, unless you change and become like little children, you will never enter the kingdom of heaven'" (Matthew 18:1-3).

Our children are great in God's kingdom. We have a lot to learn from them.

The question is: Are we willing to listen? If we are, it will help us become the fathers God wants us to be.

YOUR CHALLENGE

In their book *Sticking with Your Teen*, authors Joe White and Lissa Halls Johnson list seven ways to make sure you really hear your child, and to make sure he or she knows it:

1. *Give him your full attention.* Now isn't the time for multitasking.

2. *Reflect her emotions; don't mock them.* Sincerely mirroring those feelings on your face tells your child you understand.

3. *Restate in your own words what you heard him say.* If you restate the situation incorrectly, it gives your child a chance to re-explain.

4. *Display attentive body language.* Skip the eye rolling, sighs, and arms crossed tightly against the chest.

5. *Decide to be interested in what she's saying.* It may help to remind yourself that what you're really interested in is *her.*

6. *Listen to actions.* Pay attention when your child slams doors or leaves incriminating notes from a boyfriend or girlfriend around the house.

7. *Be alert for moments of honesty and vulnerability.* When this happens, give kids all the time they need to share.[4]

Pick one of these suggestions to try during the next 24 hours. Plan to start a conversation with a question, and to listen carefully to the result.

YOUR PLAN

What question will you use to start your conversation? Here are some ideas from Joe White and Lissa Halls Johnson:

"How is life going for you?"

"What level of your video game are you at right now? What's the most challenging thing about it?"

"How do you think basketball is going? Where do you want to improve? What does the coach say about the team's prospects?"

"What do you like best about your friend Sara?"

One question may not keep the conversation going, of course. So, in the following space, write two or three you might use to break the ice and practice listening.[5]

_____

_____

_____

_____

_____

_____

_____

■ ■ ■

WAYNE GORDON is founding pastor of Lawndale Community Church in Chicago as well as president of the Christian Community Development Association. During more than thirty-five years of ministry, "Coach," as he is affectionately known, has played a key role in numerous initiatives including the Lawndale Christian Health Center. A graduate of Wheaton College and Northern Baptist Theological Seminary, he received his doctor of ministry degree from Eastern Baptist Theological Seminary. He is the author of *Real Hope in Chicago*, a book describing God's power at work in a needy community, and *Who Is My Neighbor?*, which helps answer that question through the story of the man left for dead on the road from Jericho to Jerusalem. Wayne and his wife, Anne, have raised two sons and a daughter.

When All Is Said and Done

BY DR. KEN CANFIELD

Ponder this scenario for a moment: The end of your life is near, and you know it. You're ready to leave this world and, if you've put your faith in Christ, to join your Father in heaven. Your legacy is set, the deal is done, and during your last few days you have time to reflect on the impact of your fathering.

You think back on all those conversations with your wife, your children, and others in your family. You wonder: Were those exchanges filled with words of appreciation and praise?

I know this exercise is a bit melancholy, but play it out. From an end-of-life perspective on your fathering right now, are you leaving nothing unsaid or undone? No regrets? What words of blessing are you depositing in your family's emotional bank account? When did you make your last deposit?

We spend most of our lives checking our financial inventory, counting every dollar in the process. But how much time do we invest in praise for those we love the most? Would the negatives outweigh the positives? What's the fiscal balance of your own praise account?

Or consider this angle. If your children were asked to summarize your entire life in a phrase or sentence, what would they say? How would they describe your influence on their lives? Words and phrases become epitaphs, and epitaphs mark legacy. If your words of praise have been plentiful, positive, and focused, you're living with purpose—much as my friend Peter Spokes sought to live.

I knew Peter for many years and worked alongside him for over a decade. Our mutual goal was to inspire, equip, and strengthen fathers with tools, training, and resources. Peter was committed to excellence throughout his career, and he took the same approach in his fathering. He did whatever it took to become the best dad he could be. He latched on to the best thinking, advice, and experiences and made fathering a priority in his life.

When we traveled together, Peter would always update me on the choices each of his kids was making regarding friends, athletics, school experiences, family interaction, and faith formation. He would ask me for counsel.

He did all that because he wanted to provide the best fathering he possibly could. He wasn't perfect, but he clearly honored his father and mother, loved his wife, and sought to raise his fathering standard a couple of notches by being tuned in to each of his children.

No one but God saw Peter's sickness and death coming. In six short months, life left Peter's body.

He has a different vantage point now. I'm sure he's lifting up prayers of support and thanks for those he left behind, in sync with his Savior.

For me, his life is a reminder that we need to be sober about our fathering. If I could talk with Peter or get him a question, I would ask, "Peter, what advice would you give to fathers who are yearning to be the best dads they can be in the time they have left?"

From my experience and conversations with him over the years, here is what I think he would say: "Be lavish using words of encouragement to bless every member of your household, early and often. Begin first with your wife; make sure her cup is filled and overflows to all in the household. Second, make sure each of your children knows how proud and honored you are to be his or her father, and that the privilege of being his or her dad has been one of the greatest experiences of your life. Lastly, let words of appreciation and gratefulness be common in everyday speech and action. Constructive criticism has its place, but let it be overwhelmed with effusive praise, because you don't know how many days you have left with each of your children. You just don't know."

Psalm 90:12 tells us, "Teach us to number our days aright, that we may gain a heart of wisdom." We "number our days" by taking an eternal perspective on our earthly priorities. We stay aware that life is short and seek to invest wisely the time we have left.

How do we do that? Based on what I observed in Peter's life, here are three suggestions:

1. *Put your past into proper perspective.* Peter knew that one of the best ways to learn from childhood experiences and fill your vocabulary with words of blessing is to sift through your past and focus on the good. That's what he did. As the apostle Paul suggested, "Whatever is true, whatever is noble, whatever is right, whatever is pure, whatever is lovely, whatever is admirable—if anything is excellent or praiseworthy—think about such things . . . and the God of peace will be with you" (Philippians 4:8-9).

2. *Blaze a bold, new trail.* Peter's memories of what he wanted as a child led him to understand his own children's needs. It was his lifelong pursuit to become involved, nurturing, and encouraging as a father.

Peter became a passionate learner. People like that are always in the hunt to do the best with the tools they've been given—and to take it up a notch or two. Your fathering will be deeply influenced by the support of those around you—your child's mother, other men, family members, teachers, coaches, counselors, ministry leaders, work associates, and friends. As you seek their advice, vulnerability and honesty should be your calling cards.

3. *Keep affirming your children.* Peter knew that words have a profound impact on kids. I think he would urge you to be careful how you talk to yours. In far too many homes, without giving it a second thought, men use careless, condemning terms that propel their children toward a life of hopelessness, low self-esteem, and disrespect for others.

Even if it doesn't feel natural at first, keep trying! It's so important for your kids' confidence and sense of well-being. Resist the notion that your children need to earn your approval or live up to certain expectations before you'll say, "I'm proud of you," or "I love you." Your pride in your children and love for them should be based on who they are—nothing else.

I'm asking you to do something almost supernatural. Your father may have used words to tear you down, but you can be different. Your positive words and actions can add up to a legacy that helps set the course of your child's future—a legacy you'll never regret.

YOUR CHALLENGE

Affirming your children is an important part of your legacy. But it requires having a clear sense of the message you want to impress on them. You can't afford to speak "off the cuff" here, and they can spot any hint of insincerity.

During the next 12 hours, give that message some real consideration. Make it honest—from the heart—and personalize it for each child. Then, starting during the next 24 hours, say it over and over again. Repetition has power to change behavior. Use that principle to affirm your kids and speak destiny into their lives.

YOUR PLAN

Take inventory of your current affirmation habits by responding to these questions in the space below:

- What are three admirable qualities you saw in your father or father figures, and how are you passing them on to your children?
- What words of appreciation have you shared with—and about—your wife today?
- How do your words of blessing mesh with your demonstrations of affection for your children?
- What's the "signature phrase" you'd like your kids to remember you for?

_____

_____

_____

_____

_____

_____

_____

■ ■ ■

DR. KEN CANFIELD is founder of the National Center for Fathering, and served as its president and CEO from 1990 through 2005. He currently serves as a consultant to universities, agencies, governments, and a wide variety of community-based organizations. He has written for numerous publications, both popular and scientific, and is the author of many books including *The Heart of a Father* and *The 7 Secrets of Effective Fathers*. Ken has been interviewed on radio and TV programs like *The Oprah Winfrey Show* and *The Today Show* and is regarded as an authority on fathering skills and research. He holds a B.A. degree in philosophy from Friends University, an M.C.S. from the University of British Columbia-Regent College, and a Ph.D. in education from Kansas State University. Ken and his wife, Dee, have been married thirty-five years and have five children and six grandchildren.

NOTES

1. Authored by Josh McDowell, © 2011 Josh McDowell Ministries. Used by permission. All rights reserved.
2. Adapted from *6 Secrets to a Lasting Love* by Dr. Gary and Barbara Rosberg (Carol Stream, Ill.: Tyndale House Publishers, 2006)
3. Adapted from *52 Things Kids Need from a Dad* by Jay Payleitner (Eugene, Ore.: Harvest House Publishers, 2010)
4. Adapted from *Sticking with Your Teen* by Joe White with Lissa Halls Johnson (Carol Stream, Ill.: Focus on the Family/Tyndale House Publishers, 2006)
5. Ibid.

FOCUS ON THE FAMILY

Welcome to the Family

Whether you purchased this book, borrowed it, or received it as a gift, thanks for reading it! This is just one of many insightful, biblically based resources that Focus on the Family produces for people in all stages of life.

Focus is a global Christian ministry dedicated to helping families thrive as they celebrate and cultivate God's design for marriage and experience the adventure of parenthood. Our outreach exists to support individuals and families in the joys and challenges they face, and to equip and empower them to be the best they can be.

Through our many media outlets, we offer help and hope, promote moral values and share the life-changing message of Jesus Christ with people around the world.

Focus on the Family MAGAZINES

These faith-building, character-developing publications address the interests, issues, concerns, and challenges faced by every member of your family from preschool through the senior years.

For More INFORMATION

 ONLINE:
Log on to
FocusOnTheFamily.com
In Canada, log on to
FocusOnTheFamily.ca

 PHONE:
Call toll-free:
**800-A-FAMILY
(232-6459)**
In Canada, call toll-free:
800-661-9800

THRIVING FAMILY®	**FOCUS ON THE FAMILY CLUBHOUSE JR.®**	**FOCUS ON THE FAMILY CLUBHOUSE®**	**FOCUS ON THE FAMILY CITIZEN®**	
Marriage & Parenting	Ages 4 to 8	Ages 8 to 12	U.S. news issues	Rev. 3/11

More Great Resources
from Focus on the Family®

Essentials of Parenting: Be Prepared
Equipping Kids to Face Today's World

This DVD and CD-ROM present practical plans for dealing with dangers including Internet porn, alcohol, drugs, eating disorders, and premarital sex. You'll see how to resist the impulse to overprotect your child—and gain insights to help you prepare him or her for the world of today and tomorrow.

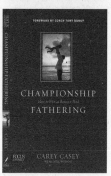

Championship Fathering:
How to Win at Being a Dad
by Carey Casey

Follow a winning game plan and rise to the top of the standings as "Best Dad"! Drawing on his experience as a parent, son, and NFL chaplain, the CEO of the National Center for Fathering reveals a life-tested "Loving, Coaching, and Modeling" strategy for raising well-adjusted and confident kids.

Losing Control & Liking It:
How to Set Your Teen (and Yourself) Free
by Tim Sanford

Feeling pressured to make your kids turn out right? Tired of trying to control them? At last, here's relief from a burden you were never meant to carry. A longtime counselor and parent helps you build family relationships based not on fear, force, or manipulation, but influence, reality, and trusting God.

Championship Fathering
A Call to Action

You've read about the crisis of fatherlessness and the negative consequences for children and for our society. Even if you're an involved dad, your children and grandchildren will grow up in a culture full of unfathered kids, and they will be affected!

Dads are a critical part of the solution, but we have to get involved. For the sake of our children and grandchildren and millions of other kids, we need to stand up and be counted.

The National Center for Fathering is calling every dad to make a commitment to practice the five elements of *Championship Fathering*: loving his children, coaching his children, modeling for his children, encouraging other children, and enlisting other men to join the *Championship Fathering* team.

Our goal is to recruit 6.5 million fathers—equal to 10 percent of the fathers in America. That's enough dads standing shoulder-to-shoulder to span the country from Boston to San Diego. We believe it's enough to create a culture of *Championship Fathering* and positively influence our children's future. We hope this vision challenges and inspires you to act now.

Make a difference, dad. Get in the game! Begin to live the principles of *Championship Fathering* today and let us know about it by registering your commitment at www.fathers.com/go.

fathers.com
NATIONAL CENTER FOR FATHERING

About the National Center for Fathering

Our vision is that every child would have an involved father or father figure—that no child would go unfathered.

That vision begins with the conviction that every child needs a dad he or she can count on. We know that children thrive when they have an involved father—someone who loves them, knows them, guides them, and helps them achieve their destiny.

Motivated by this heartfelt conviction and encompassing vision, the Center's board, employees, and volunteers work to inspire and equip men to make and live out a commitment to Championship Fathering by focusing on three core activities: reaching, teaching, and unleashing dads.

Reaching Dads

Reaching dads starts by connecting with men where they're at physically, emotionally, and spiritually in their fathering journey. We do this through programs like WATCH D.O.G.S., our school-based father involvement program, where dads spend a day volunteering in their kids' school. As of this writing, programs are in more than 2,100 schools, involving more than 200,000 dads and touching the lives of over 1.1 million children. In addition, we reach dads through a variety of speaking and teaching venues: churches, civic organizations, pro sports teams, business, and professional conferences. Through our *Today's Father* radio program and podcasts we touch thousands of listeners daily. Our Father of the Year essay contests have reached more than 1,000,000 dads over the past 18 years through the compelling words of their children.

Teaching Dads

Many of the current generation of fathers have grown up without adequate models of how to fulfill their role as fathers. Some dads need a little teaching; some need a lot. We equip them with the knowledge and tools they need to be the fathers their children need. We use research-based tools delivered through conferences, small groups, books, and online resources. Our Personal Fathering Profile helps dads measure their fathering behaviors and attitudes. These efforts are multiplied by a network of trainers in communities across the country who have been equipped at workshops and conferences conducted by NCF.

Unleashing Dads

Our goal is to lead a movement to change the culture of fathering in America, but we know we can't do it alone. That's why it's absolutely critical to unleash dads to live Championship Fathering for their own kids, encourage and mentor fatherless kids in their neighborhoods, and enlist other men to do the same. Only by challenging dads to reach out beyond their own families can we hope to see a changed culture.

To learn more about the National Center for Fathering and how you can get involved in helping create a culture of Championship Fathering, visit our Web site at www.fathers.com.

FREE Discussion Guide!

Reproducible discussion questions

for this book are available at: www.tyndale.com